SHALOM TORAH CENTERS

מוסדות שלום לחינוך ילדים

SHALOM TORAH CENTERS: EDUCATING GENERATIONS

Just across the Hudson River, close to the dynamic Jewish centers of New York City, lies the State of New Jersey. Except for a few enclaves of strong Jewish awareness, crossing this river is like crossing into another world. For the more than a half million Jews residing in cities and suburban towns across New Jersey, traditional Judaism may, unfortunately, become something of the past. Their children, conveniently blended into the local public school system, will never be given the opportunity to discover the singular beauty of our Torah, its heritage and traditions. At worst, these Jewish children will intermarry and be forever lost to our people. At best, they will carry their Jewishness through life as an unwelcome burden, and their own children will be that much further from the rest of us. We stand today–literally–facing the disappearance of thousands of families from our nation, unless we can reach out and pull them back from oblivion.

In a courageous effort, a group of Torah scholars from Beth Medrash Govoha in Lakewood, New Jersey, joined together in the early seventies to create the Shalom Torah Centers. Although committed to spreading the light of Torah to all the Jewish people of New Jersey, Shalom Torah Centers began with the children.

The first Shalom Torah Center, an afternoon Hebrew school, was established in Manalapan Township in 1973 with an enrollment of thirty-one children. Viewed from the perspective of the overall situation, it was a nick in a mountainous problem, but it was a beginning nonetheless. Viewed from an individual perspective, however, it represented thirty-one victories, for every Jewish child is priceless in its own right. Every Jewish child carries with it the prayers and sacrifices of countless generations of its forebears and the hope for all future generations.

Looking back, the first twenty years have been a time of growth and consolidation for Shalom Torah Centers. That first small school has grown into a blossoming network of four Talmud Torahs (Manalapan,

East Windsor, Matawan, South Brunswick), two Hebrew day schools that collectively reach hundreds of Jewish children, a *shul*, and a highly effective and comprehensive Adult Education program. What began as an initiative to reach out and save our children has actually come full circle with the founding and growth of the Adult Education division.

In Twin Rivers, the Morris Namias Shalom Torah Academy is credited with transforming an entire community, providing a beautiful Orthodox *shul*, excellent education for the children in a Torah-oriented environment and a full program of adult education courses. The Shalom Torah Academy of Englishtown-Old Bridge has also exprienced phenomenal growth while assuming the role of a much needed center for both children's and adult education.

Currently, close to 100 members, men and women of Shalom communities, meet on a weekly basis with scholars of the Lakewood community to study Torah and learn about *Yiddishkeit* on a one to one basis. This dynamic *Chavrusa* program has grown to include five communities, with sessions taking place every night of the week and many of the participants and their families becoming fully observant. A new series of lunchtime classes and adult seminars has recently begun to great acclaim.

It is well known that most people drift away from the Torah and traditional Jewish values only because of ignorance. They need only be reached and they will respond. At Shalom Torah Centers, this has been proven on all levels. Whether at a *Shabbaton* weekend, an adult seminar, a weekly study session, or during the daily school curriculum, it can be seen in the profound and genuine delight that lights up the eyes of our fellow Jews as they discover the heritage that is rightfully theirs.

As Shalom Torah Centers face the future, they can point proudly to their record of achievements. They have emerged as a major force in the battle against the tide of assimilation in America. The present network of schools and programs continues to blossom; the quality of the education in both Torah related and secular subjects is uniformly excellent; parent and community response is enthusiastic. Indeed, a strong nucleus has been created; yet for every child and adult reached by Shalom Torah Centers, there are thousands more to be reached in communities across New Jersey and its neighboring states.

Yes, the future unfolds with great promise, provided, however, that there is a major investment of long hours, hard work, and new resources.

In the Footsteps of the Prophets

of the Prophets

A Treasury of Midrashic Chronicles

The Shalom Tanach Series

Volume Four
The Period of the Kings

In the Footsteps of the Prophets

A Treasury of Midrashic Chronicles

A *revised excerpt from*
Rabbi Yisroel Yaakov Klapholtz's
The Nach Treasury

C.I.S. PUBLISHERS

New York • London • Jerusalem

The incidents and events in this book are all recorded and described in *Midrashim* and *Gemara*. The exact wording of description and dialogue is that of the current author, but in keeping with *Midrashic* accounts.

Special excerpt published by
C.I.S. Publishers and Distributors
180 Park Avenue
Lakewood, New Jersey 08701
(908) 905-3000
Fax: (908) 367-6666

Published with special permission by
Mishor Publishing Company
800 Wythe Avenue
Brooklyn, New York 11211

Book and cover design: Deenee Cohen
Typography: Nechamie Miller
Cover illustration: Francis McGinley

ISBN 1-56062-274-1

PRINTED IN THE UNITED STATES OF AMERICA

TABLE OF CONTENTS

PART THREE-YONAH THE PROPHET

Part One

THE KINGS OF JUDAH AND ISRAEL

THE JEWISH MONARCHY · A TIMELINE

KINGS OF ISRAEL	YEARS
Saul ben Kish	2
Ish Boshes ben Saul	2
David ben Jesse	40
Solomon ben David	40

KINGS OF JUDAH	
Rehoboam ben Solomon	17
Abiah ben Rehoboam	3
Asa ben Abiah	41
Jehoshafat ben Asa	25
Jehoram ben Jehoshafat	8
Achaziah ben Jehoram	1
Athaliah, mother of Achaziah	6
Jehoash ben Achaziah	40
Amaziah ben Jehoash	29
Uzziahu (Azariah) ben Amaziah	52
Josam ben Uzziahu	16
Achaz ben Josam	16
Chizkiyahu ben Achaz	29
Menashe ben Chizkiyahu	56
Ammon ben Menashe	2
Yoshiahu ben Ammon	31
Yehoachaz ben Yoshiahu	3 Months
Yehoyakim ben Yoshiahu	11
Yehoyachim ben Yehoyakim	3 Months
Zidkiyahu ben Yoshiahu	11

KINGS OF ISRAEL (10 TRIBES)	
Jeroboam ben Nebat	22
Nadab ben Jerboam	2
Ba'sha ben Achiah	24
Elah ben Ba'sha	2
Zimri	7 Days
Amri	12
Ahab ben Imri	22
Achaziah ben Ahab	2
Yehoram ben Ahab	12
Yehu ben Nimshi	28
Yehoachaz ben Yehu	17
Yehoash ben Yehoachaz	16
Jeroboam ben Yehoash	41
Zechariah ben Jeroboam	6 Months
Shallum ben Yabesh	1 Month
Menachem ben Gadi	10
Pekachiah ben Menachem	2
Pekach ben Remaliahu	20
Hoshea ben Elah	19

1

SHLOMO'S KINGDOM IS SPLIT

King Shlomo had many wives. One of them, Pharaoh's daughter, was not satisfied with the vast riches she enjoyed at the palace. She demanded more and more. Towards the end of his days, the king could no longer withstand her constant badgering and would give in to her requests. He gave her servants and maids without number, until there was no room in the palace to put them all. So she begged Shlomo to build special housing for her servants and maids. The king ordered these quarters built in Milo, between Jerusalem and Zion, which his father David had set aside for the *olei regel*.

When the *olei regel* came on their pilgrimages, they were incensed at the sight of these buildings which had taken over their prime place of lodging. One in particular, Yeravam ben Nevat, who would one day become king himself, came before the king and said, "Your father especially opened up the city walls to make it more accessible for us, the *olei regel*. What did you do? You blocked off our roads, forcing people to enter the city only through the special gates in the wall. You did it for your own sake so that you could take tolls from people who entered the city and use the money for the various caprices of your wife, Pharaoh's daughter." These words angered the king, and he sought to punish Yeravam, but the latter fled in time.

When Yeravam fled from the king, he met up with the prophet Achiya Hashiloni, who told him, "I am informing you that Hashem has chosen you to rule over the Jewish people. If you want your kingdom and your dynasty to last for many generations to come, you must obey Hashem's commands and walk the path of righteousness without deviating."

After Shlomo's death the Kingdom of Israel was split in two; the Kingdom of Judah was made up of the tribes of Yehudah and Binyamin, while the Kingdom of Israel was made up of the remaining ten tribes. King David had been given a hint of this development after he said to Shaul's grandson, Mefiboshes, whom he suspected of disloyalty, "You and Tziva are to divide the field." At this time a heavenly voice announced, "Since you did not check into the words of Tziva who really lied when he said that his master, Mefiboshes, was disloyal, you will be punished. Your kingdom will be torn in two. Yeravam ben Nevat will rule one half, while your grandson Rechavam will rule the other."

2

YERAVAM BEN NEVAT

Yeravam ben Nevat was the son of Sheva ben Bichri, who had rebelled against King David. Sheva had been convinced that he should rule, not realizing that what he saw prophetically was the reign of his son.

Why was he called Nevat? Because he had seen (*hibit*) a vision but interpreted it incorrectly. When Yeravam opposed King Shlomo by complaining about the servants' quarters he had built for Pharaoh's daughter upon the land that had been used by the *olei regel*, Hashem said, "Who are you to scold the king? He is the most honored person in the entire nation. I will give you only a part of his kingdom and responsibilities, and we will see how you fare. You will not be able to stand the pressures."

Yeravam ben Nevat was the disciple of the prophet Achiya Hashiloni. Achiya was a complete *tzaddik*, one of the pillars of the world. He stemmed from the tribe of Levi and enjoyed an especially long life. He had been born sixty years before the Jews left Egypt and continued to live until the era of the kings. He was so unusually great that Rabbi Shimon bar Yochai used to say, "My merit and the merit of Achiya Hashiloni combined are enough to protect all the generations from the times of Avraham to the *Mashiach*." Even as a youth, Yeravam was extremely well-versed in Torah, almost as thoroughly as his master, Achiya. He knew it backwards and forwards, and it flowed from his mouth like honey. So great were this master and *talmid* that in comparison, all the scholars of that generation were like so much grass.

One time, when Achiya and Yeravam were studying the secrets of the Torah together, the angels came before Hashem and said, "Master of the universe! To this man, who we know will later erect two golden calves for idol worship—to this man You reveal the secrets of the Divine chariot and other esoteric matters?"

"What is he doing right now?" Hashem replied.

"Right now he is purely righteous; he is studying Torah," they answered.

"I am the Divine Judge. I judge a person according to his present behavior, not by what he will do some day in the future. If he is upright now, I cannot punish him for future deeds." Nevertheless, Hashem considered removing Yeravam from the world before he sinned, for He knew that those sins would be terrible indeed, and the punishment for them too awful to bear. Hashem turned to the Angel of Death and said, "Go and bring Me the soul of Yeravam ben Nevat." When the angels heard this order they hurriedly presented themselves before Hashem and begged, "Hashem, our Master! How mighty is Your Name throughout the world! You are different from human kings. Your justice lies in the fact that You are long-suffering and do not punish people until they actually sin. At this very moment, Yeravam is still righteous. Let him be." Hashem gave in, "I will do as you suggest, but know that he will be a terrible sinner."

When Yeravam gained the throne and all the honor that went along with it, he forgot Hashem Who had elevated him and put the royal scepter in his hand. He abandoned the G-d of Israel and began worshipping man-made idols. He erected two golden calves and misled the people into worshipping them. He would not allow the people to go to Jerusalem, to the Beis Hamikdash, for he feared that Rechavam ben Shlomo, King of Judah, would gain their loyalty. King Yeravam and his subjects worshipped their idols, forgetting all about Hashem. To the angels, Hashem said, "Do you see what Yeravam has done? All the wealth and power which I bestowed upon him was diverted to idol worship! Would it not have been for him to die while he was still righteous? Had he come to heaven he would have been able to learn Torah from the angels. Now he will have to go to Gehinnom."

3

RECHAVAM BEN SHLOMO

After King Shlomo's death, his son Rechavam succeeded to the throne. This son was not righteous like his grandfather, David, or his father, Shlomo. On the contrary, he was evil, and light-minded as well.

Rechavam soon lost a large portion of his kingdom. While this had been already decreed by Hashem, Rechavam himself caused the people to hate him.

When he first assumed the throne, the representatives of the people asked him to lessen the tax burden which his father had imposed.

The king's elderly advisors suggested to the young king that he give in to the request of the masses, thus gaining their confidence and respect. But the young king preferred to listen to his friends, idlers and base people like himself. They advised him instead to increase taxes and give the following reply to the delegation, "My father punished you with whips. I will torture you with scorpions."

And he did. He gathered all the people together and publicly announced, "I am your king. You must obey me. I demand that you bring me more and more gold. If my father's demands were harsh, mine will be ever so much harsher!"

Stunned and disappointed, the people left the gathering. And when Yeravam ben Nevat came along and suggested that, unlike the unbending Rechavam, he would be a merciful and loving king, they accepted him eagerly and followed him joyfully.

4

THE REIGN OF YERAVAM BEN NEVAT

Yeravam wished to have tight control over the nation. But he first had to win the people's confidence. He therefore gathered their leaders at a meeting to which he also invited his wicked friends. He seated them alternately, *tzaddik* next to sinner. Then he asked, "Do I please you as king?" They all answered, "Yes." He continued, "Will you obey all that I demand and fulfill all I command?" They agreed to do so. He then continued, "What if I told you to worship idols and abandon Hashem? Would you obey me in this respect too?" The *tzaddikim* at this gathering were shocked and cried out, "Never! We would not leave Hashem, our G-d, Who created heaven and earth." But the sinners, seated among them, turned to their neighbors on each side and began inciting them to listen to Yeravam. They laughed at their fears and said cunningly, "Did you really think that Yeravam had that in mind? Don't you know him as a righteous and learned scholar? He was only testing you to see how loyal you were to Hashem." The *tzaddikim* were taken in by this smooth argument and agreed that he would make a fine king.

But Yeravam was not satisfied with their word alone. Wishing to be absolutely sure of his power, he forced them to sign a document which read, "Yeravam ben Nevat is King of Israel. We shall obey all he tells us." The *tzaddikim* among them were afraid to commit themselves in writing, and went first to ask the advice of Achiya Hashiloni. Because Achiya knew that Hashem intended Yeravam to rule, he told them that they should sign the declaration of loyalty to the new king. On the day that they signed their allegiance to Yeravam, he was crowned over the ten tribes of Israel. Joy and jubilation filled the hearts of the people. There was feasting and celebration, drinking and toasting. Little did the people know that their new king would lead them down the path of destruction.

That very evening, the wicked friends of the king came and demanded that he allow them to publicly worship idols as he had suggested. This is what Yeravam really wanted, but he was afraid that these people were making their request out of drunken confusion, and when they sobered up, they would regret what they had done. "Come to me tomorrow," he suggested. Yeravam wanted them to sin with clear heads and sober intentions, not out of drunken confusion. When they came to him on the following day, he said, "If you really wish that I erect large temples and idols, you must decide to reject the elders of the *Sanhedrin*. You must not go to them to be judged and not heed what they say." The people agreed to this.

From that time on, Yeravam sinned more and more, dragging the people down with him. He sent his wicked friends to every Jewish settlement to persuade them to abandon Hashem and worship idols. These messengers used to ask the people, "Which generation do you admire most?" They would reply, "The generation of the desert." This would give the inciters a perfect opening, "Then let us follow their

19

example! They made a golden calf and bowed down before it. Let us do the same!" They went from family to family, inciting them to worship idols.

And still this wicked king was not satisfied. Before *Sukkos* at the end of the *shemitah* year, Yeravam hatched a terrible plan. Realizing that the Jews would go to Jerusalem for the special *mitzvah* of *hakheil*—when the King of Judah read the Torah before the entire nation—he feared that they would transfer their allegiance back to Rechavam. And he knew that if he himself went, he would be regarded as Rechavam's subject, not as an equal. He would not be allowed to sit down, for sitting was the sole privilege of the kings of the House of David. If he stood, the people would think him no better than they. If he sat, this would be considered treason, and he would be killed. He therefore decided to ban his subjects from going to Jerusalem altogether.

He made two golden calves and erected them in two separate places. "If the Jews wish to offer sacrifices," he declared, "they could do so to these golden images." The king stationed soldiers on all roads leading to Jerusalem to prevent people from going. Indeed, the king himself was the first to offer sacrifices to the golden calves. Not satisfied with his wickedness, he abolished all the Jewish holidays and festivals, and instituted new ones instead. He even uprooted the *Shabbos* and claimed to change the laws of the Torah. Every single wicked thought that entered his mind was carried out. And there was no pleasure that he did not indulge in.

Hashem would sometimes call his attention to the possibility of doing *teshuvah*. The king would hear a heavenly voice speaking to him, "Return, Yeravam, to Hashem. Why should you perish in the fires of Gehinnom?" But Yeravam ignored the voice which called to him. Once Hashem seized Yeravam by the coat and said, "Repent! Do *teshuvah* and I will walk with you and (David) ben Yishai in Gan Eden." The arrogant king asked, "Who will be first?" On hearing that ben Yishai would precede him, Yeravam was insulted. He replied, "If so, I am not interested. I will not return."

5

YERAVAM AND THE MAN OF G-D

One time, while Yeravam was busy sacrificing to his golden calves, he was approached by the prophet Ido who had been sent by Hashem. When he saw the king in the midst of his sinful activity, he began prophesying, "Woe unto you, O altar! The day will come when a son will be born to the House of David. Yoshiyahu will be his name. He will destroy all the priests of the Baal and will bring sacrifices upon the altar of Hashem. The day will come when the bones of a human being will be burnt upon you."

These frightening words shook the people who were present. They realized that this foretold the bitter end of Yeravam, but out of respect for the king's position, Ido had not mentioned his name specifically. The king was also aware that he was the object of this prophecy. In his anger, he stretched his hand out to grab the prophet and punish him. But just then his hand became paralyzed. The king looked at his useless limb and begged the prophet to forgive him and to pray to Hashem to heal it. Instead of being vengeful, Ido went ahead and prayed that Hashem restore the use of Yeravam's hand. And lo, before everyone's eyes, the hand became normal again. But in spite of this wondrous miracle, the king did not repent. He continued sacrificing to his idols while the people joined him in idol worship.

Wishing to express his thanks, the king invited the prophet to the palace for a feast, but the latter refused. "Even if you gave me half of your palace, I would not eat from your table," he said, for Hashem had commanded him to return to his home.

Among the people who had witnessed the amazing miracle were sons of a false prophet. After Ido left, they went to their father and told them what had happened. This false prophet hurried after Ido and when he overtook him, begged that he join him in a meal. But Ido refused on the same grounds; Hashem had commanded him to return home. "But I am a prophet just like you," said the man. "An angel appeared to me and commanded me in the Name of Hashem to invite you to eat with me." Ido believed this false prophet and accompanied him home. He ate, drank and rested up from his journey. Because the false prophet hosted him with such genuine respect, he was rewarded with true prophecy. Before the man of Hashem parted, his host said, "Since you believed me and did not obey the word of G-d forbidding you to eat and drink in this place, you will be punished. You will not be buried together with your ancestors."

Ido left and continued his journey. Along the road, far from any settlement, he was suddenly attacked by a hungry lion who pounced upon him. The lion killed him but would not touch his flesh; he also left Ido's donkey untouched. The next day the false prophet learned of the misfortune and came searching for Ido's remains. He found the lion crouching over the prophet's body and the donkey standing by, unharmed.

Amazed and deeply moved, the false prophet thought to himself, "Hashem is righteous in all of His ways. Behold the lion, who does not receive reward or punishment for his deeds, fulfilling the command of his Creator, standing guard over the body which he had been commanded to kill. Not only that, he even left the donkey untouched although he was starving! How much more so must man be careful to obey Hashem, for he receives reward and punishment for his deeds." The false prophet then took the body, carried it to his city and buried it with the utmost respect. Then he said to his sons, "When I die, I wish to be buried next to this holy man."

6

YERAVAM AND RECHAVAM

Yeravam was not satisfied with the ten tribes that he ruled.
Drunk with power, he wished to banish Rechavam ben
Shlomo from his throne and rule the tribes of Yehudah and
Binyamin as well. He called his military leaders together and
said, "Let us declare war upon Rechavam and upon Jerusalem." The heads of the ten tribes refused. "Why should we do
this?" they asked. "Why should we make war on the son of our
beloved King Shlomo and on the residents of Jerusalem, our
brothers!"

Seeing that they disagreed with him, the king called
together the elders and told them to select one particular tribe,
who would have to produce soldiers to fight this war for the
king. The elders recommended the tribe of Dan, whose men
were the strongest and bravest of all. They would obey their
king even if they disagreed with him about starting a war. This
advice pleased Yeravam. He summoned the leaders of Dan
and told them to prepare for war against Judah. The tribesmen
were shocked. They did not wish to fight against their own
brothers! "How can we shed innocent blood?" they asked in
horror. They were ready to stand on this principle and defy
their king rather than fight against their innocent brothers.

Their readiness for self-sacrifice pleased Hashem. And thus, a civil war between Yeravam and Rechavam was averted.

In time, Yeravam did wage war against the king of Judah. Although neither side really won, both sides refused to make peace. And so a state of war continued to exist between the two kingdoms. This strife should have taken place between David and Sheva ben Bichri, but Hashem had said, "The Beis Hamikdash has not yet been built. Shall I allow a civil war in the midst of My people and stand for rebellion against the kingdom of David? No. I shall wait until the Beis Hamikdash is built. Then, let come what may." Indeed, throughout the period of kings, the two kingdoms were constantly at odds with one another. There was no peace as each kingdom tried unsuccessfully to subdue the other.

7

AVIYA BEN YERAVAM

One of Yeravam's sons, Aviya, was not a sinner like his father. He never bowed to his father's golden calves and disobeyed his father's law against going to Jerusalem. Each time he had a chance, he secretly went to the House of Hashem, prayed there and returned home. Yeravam learned of his son's disobedience and scolded him, but this did not prevent Aviya from stealing away again to Jerusalem to pray to Hashem. He also assisted the relatively small number of Jews who opposed Yeravam's ways to journey to Jerusalem. Being the son of the king, Aviya was able to tell the border patrol to look aside while he crossed over. The guards never said a word. He was their prince, and they felt obligated to obey him. When these soldiers left their posts temporarily, Aviya would open the border to all those who wanted to go up to Jerusalem.

One time Aviya fell ill. Concerned, Yeravam told his wife to go to the man who had crowned him, Achiya Hashiloni, and ask him what will be with the child. Yeravam did not tell his wife to pray to the golden calves but to go to the man of G-d, for he realized that only Hashem had the power of life and death. Yeravam was clever enough to know that if Achiya recognized the queen, he would surely not agree to pray for the son of such terrible sinners. He therefore told her to disguise herself. Also, he did not want his subjects to say that the king rejected his idols in his time of need and sought the help of the true prophet for his ailing son.

Not long afterward, the prophet heard the sound of approaching footsteps. Very old and feeble, he could no longer see, but Hashem revealed to him who had come. Achiya called out to her, "Enter, wife of Yeravam! Why have you disguised yourself? Draw near and hear the word of Hashem. Go and tell your husband, Yeravam, thus, 'Hashem raised you above the entire nation and chose you to be king over Israel. But you were ungrateful. You abandoned Hashem and pursued ways of emptiness and vanity. You worshipped man-made idols of wood and stone. Even though you were warned to observe Hashem's *mitzvos*, you did not follow the example of David. Therefore, says Hashem, you will be severely punished. All of your family will be destroyed. Not a trace will remain. They will not die a normal death but will be cruelly killed. Nor will they be given a decent burial. Those of your clan who die in the city will be eaten by dogs, while those who die in the fields will be devoured by birds of prey.'"

Then the prophet added, "You have come asking mercy for your son Aviya. Know that Hashem has already taken pity on him. But how? Hashem will gather his soul to Him. Aviya will not get up from his sickbed, but he will be granted an honorable burial. Indeed, of the entire House of Yeravam, only he will merit burial."

Disappointed, the queen returned to the palace. Just as her foot crossed the threshold, the prophet's prediction came true.

On the very day that Aviya died, his wife gave birth to a son. This son was secretly taken away from the palace to the desert. He grew up there among a group of a hundred and seventy people from the tribe of Ephraim. These people had not sinned along with Yeravam ben Nevat but had been loyal to Hashem all these years. The boy was raised in the way of the Torah and became a *tzaddik* like his teachers. In the latter days, one of his descendants will prove to be *Mashiach ben Yosef*. He will lead battles to deliver his people, preparing the way for the ultimate redeemer, *Mashiach ben David*.

8

AVIYA BEN RECHAVAM

After the death of Rechavam ben Shlomo, his son Aviya mounted the throne of the Kingdom of Judah. He followed in his father's footsteps by doing evil. He ignored the Torah, pursuing idolatry instead. Not only did he sin against Hashem, he also sinned against his fellow man by treating his subjects cruelly. Like his father, he hated Yeravam, who had taken away ten tribes and split his kingdom in two. While Yeravam had tried unsuccessfully to start a war against Rechavam—no Jewish soldier was willing to fight against his brothers—he did succeed in waging war against Rechavam's son Aviya.

Aviya's cruelty was revealed in this civil war, which claimed many victims from the ten tribes. Aviya would not allow these bodies to be buried. He posted guards, who made sure that the bodies would rot in the fields. The widows of these fallen soldiers used to come crying to the king, "What will become of us? Our husbands have died, we know, but their bodies lie rotting in the fields and cannot even be identified. Now we can never prove that they died and must remain living widows to the end of our lives!" While full of sympathy, the Jewish sages had no choice but to agree that they could not remarry.

"As long as there are no witnesses to testify to their death and no one to identify them," they said, "you are forbidden to marry again." That infamous war produced many such *agunos*, women who remained alone to the end of their days, weeping at their tragic fate.

The Jews of Yehudah and Binyamin did not want to fight against their brothers of the ten tribes. Aviya drafted them into his army through trickery, pretending that he was fighting for a righteous cause. "If we win," he said, "we will be able to destroy the golden calves Yeravam made for idolatry." Aviya won this war but did not keep his promise. A sinner, he lasted on the throne for three years, only in the merit of his grandfather, David, to whose seed Hashem had promised the rule forevermore.

9

ASA, KING OF JUDAH

Asa was the son of Aviya, but he was not a sinner like his father. A G-d-fearing man, he ruled over his kingdom for forty-one years. A brave warrior, he was exceptionally fleet-footed. Hashem had blessed him with strong, speedy legs so that he might serve Him all the better. The king did much to direct his people in the right way. He destroyed all of the idols which his father had erected and burned the statue which his mother had made, dispersing the ashes in the Kidron stream. Hashem was pleased with Asa's actions and rewarded him with victories over all his enemies.

In a war against the Cushites, Asa was victorious and gained much war booty. Among the treasures which his soldiers took from the Cushites was the legendary throne of his great-grandfather Shlomo, as well as many treasures of gold and silver which the Cushites had seized from Judah in the time of Yeravam. But Asa's victory was short-lived, for soon afterwards, his kingdom was attacked by Baash, King of Israel. Fearing that if he lost the war, he would also lose all the treasures which he had retrieved from the Cushites, including Shlomo's throne, Asa sent these to King Haddad of Aram for safekeeping. He also asked Haddad for assistance. This displeased Hashem, for it showed Asa's lack of faith. Hashem sent the prophet Chanani to rebuke him for this.

"You have done wrong," said the prophet. "Why did you place your trust in the king of Aram? Did Hashem not grant you victory over the Cushites, who are far stronger and more numerous than the ten tribes? Had you shown that you trust in Hashem wholeheartedly and seek only His help, He would have delivered all of your enemies into your hands. Therefore, not only will you lose this battle, but all the treasures which you sent on to Aram will never return to you. Furthermore, the king of Aram will no longer be your ally, even though you flattered him with your trust." These harsh words of rebuke angered the king. He ordered his servants to seize the prophet and imprison him.

From this day on, Asa was not the same *tzaddik* that he had once been. He mobilized a huge army to fight against the ten tribes, even drafting the Torah scholars, who should have been exempt. Anyone who dared dissent or object was severely punished.

In the end of his days the king began suffering from terrible pains which began in his feet. His entire body hurt, but he still did not repent or pray to Hashem for mercy. He summoned the greatest physicians and asked them to prescribe medicines, but nothing helped. Because he did not appeal to the divine Doctor, he died in terrible pain. Before his death, Asa committed an additional sin. He married his son Yehoshafat to the daughter of Amri, the wicked King of Israel.

Asa's suffering was not the only punishment he received on account of his sins. Originally, Hashem had decreed the

split in the kingdom of David for the thirty-six years following Shlomo's death. These years ended in Asa's reign. Had
Asa been upright to the end of his days, all of the tribes would
have been reunited under one single ruler, but since Asa had
displeased Hashem, the split continued on after his death.

Part Two

ELIYAHU
AND
ELISHA

1

ACHAV, KING OF ISRAEL

An overbearing king, Achav ben Amri, sat on the throne for twenty-two years. From the magnificent palace he built himself in Shomron, the capital, he ruled over the ten tribes. Achav was a thorough sinner who did more evil than any of the other kings before him. Not only did he worship idols, but to advertise his lack of faith, he even inscribed the following on the doors of all the houses in Shomron, "Achav denies the existence of Hashem." He married Izevel bas Esbaal, King of Tzidon, and built a special temple for all the idols that she brought along from home.

Haughty and arrogant, Achav was most particular about his appearance. He wore the costliest, most fashionable clothing. Each day he would ask Chiel, his friend and courtier, "Am I not the most handsome creature in all of Israel? Don't I look beautiful today?" And Chiel would answer with flattery, "There is no one like you, Your Majesty. And when you go to worship the Baal, you will be even more splendid."

Achav was a pleasure seeker. He also desired international fame and recognition. Indeed, his appetite for honor was insatiable. Achav won the wars which he waged and demanded tribute from all the nations he subdued. He posted his own men in all of the conquered cities to inform him if anyone was planning to rebel. If the king uncovered any such plot, he would attack at once, killing many of the rebels. He would also take their sons into captivity as hostages to make sure that they would not rebel again.

In Achav's time, the entire Jewish people sinned. They abandoned Hashem's Torah and stopped believing in Hashem's Providence over the world. Chiel, the king's friend, was one of the worst inciters. He decided to rebuild the city of Jericho which had been destroyed by Yehoshua, even though the Jewish leader had put a curse on anyone who would dare rebuild it. When Chiel undertook the reconstruction, his firstborn Avirom, died. And when its gates were hinged on, the sign of completion, his youngest son, Seguv, died. Indeed, all of his sons died during the rebuilding of Jericho, but Chiel paid no attention to the heavenly warnings, nor regretted his deeds.

Hashem sent Eliyahu Hanavi to offer condolences when Chiel was mourning the death of his sons. The prophet said to Hashem, "Master of the universe! How can I go to the house of this sinner who disregarded Your command and rebuilt Jericho? If I come before him, he will curse me and You. I could not bear that!"

Hashem bade him go nevertheless. "If he does begin cursing when he sees you, and you answer him in anger, I will fulfill all that you say," Hashem promised.

Eliyahu found the king in Chiel's house. Both of them were studying Torah, discussing the curse that Yehoshua had put on the one who would dare to rebuild Jericho. When they noticed Eliyahu in the doorway, they invited him to enter. The king asked, "Tell me, who is greater, Moshe or Yehoshua?" Eliyahu replied, "The master is certainly greater than his disciple." This is what Achav had been waiting for. He said derisively, "If Moshe was so great, why was his prophecy not fulfilled? In the Torah he said, 'Beware lest your hearts stray and you worship false gods . . . Hashem will become wrathful with you and will restrain the heavens from giving rain.' Surely you know that we worship idols. There is no god before whom I have not bowed down. I have filled this land with these statues and caused everyone to sacrifice to them. Yet, not only have I not been punished, but all kinds of good things have happened to us. I have been victorious in all of my wars. Rains fall on time, and the land produces its bounty. As for the curse that Yehoshua put on the man who would dare rebuild Jericho, that has been entirely fulfilled. See, all of Chiel's sons have died. How can you say then that the master is greater than his disciple?"

Eliyahu was incensed by these blasphemous words, and deeply pained by the disgracing of Moshe, father of all prophets and leader of the people. He burst out, "It was Hashem's great mercy that spared you and let the rains fall until now. But from now on, because of your disgraceful words, years of famine will come upon the land. I swear that rain will not fall until I decree it." With these words, Eliyahu turned and left, angry and disgusted. And his dire prophecy was fulfilled in its entirety.

The famine which resulted from the drought was heavy. Achav knew that Hashem was carrying out the decree of His prophet, so he sent his servants to search for Eliyahu. Fearing the king's wrath, Eliyahu hid at the stream of Cris near the

Jordan River. He drank its waters and was fed by ravens, which brought him food twice a day from the royal table of Yehoshafat, King of Judah. Hashem had specifically instructed the ravens to take food from Yehoshafat's table rather than Achav's so that the righteous prophet would not have to get any benefit from the wicked king of Israel.

2

ELIYAHU AND THE KEY TO THE RAINS

For a long time no rain fell. The land dried up and could not produce anything. People hungered for food and thirsted for water, but there was no one to turn to for help. Even though the Jews had sinned and deserved such a punishment, Hashem, the Merciful One, had pity on them. He decided that the time had come to remove the key to the rains from Eliyahu's possession and to send rain so that the people and animals would not perish. What did he do? He dried up the stream from which Eliyahu had been drinking so that Eliyahu himself would have to pray for rain. But this did not happen. When this stream dried up, Eliyahu picked himself up and went looking for another stream.

"Rise and go to Tzarfas and remain there," Hashem commanded Eliyahu. "There you will find a certain widow, whom I have commanded to feed you." Eliyahu reached the city but did not know which woman he was supposed to seek. He therefore decided on a way to identify her. "The woman who offers to give me water must be the person whom Hashem intended." Shortly, a woman who had been gathering firewood approached him. Eliyahu asked her if she had some water for him. She quickly filled her pitcher and handed it to him. "This is the woman who is supposed to provide for me," Eliyahu thought and said aloud, "Could I have a bit of bread to revive my soul, for I am famished? I have not eaten all day."

The good woman dearly wanted to give the hungry man some food but did not have anything herself. "I swear that I do not even have a baked crust for myself," she apologized. "All I have at home is a handful of flour and a bit of oil. I came here looking for some branches to light a fire and bake a small loaf for my son and me. When that is gone, we will have nothing. If Hashem does not take pity on us, we will surely die of hunger."

Eliyahu said, "Hurry home and knead the remaining flour and oil. Bake it into a small loaf and bring it here for me. You and your son will eat afterwards."

The woman did not hesitate. She rushed home to do the prophet's bidding. Her degree of self-sacrifice greatly pleased Hashem. She did not even know this stranger, yet was ready to give him her last crust of bread, knowing that nothing would remain for herself or her son. "Since she did this," Hashem had said, "the flour and the oil in her vessels will not run out until rain falls, and the ground once more produces food."

Hashem's blessing came true, of course. This good woman and her son no longer suffered from hunger. Full of gratitude, the woman from Tzarfas begged Eliyahu to remain with her. She fed him generously all the time that he stayed there. After some time, this good woman's son became ill and died. The widow came rushing to Eliyahu, her dead son in her arms, weeping, "Why did you come here to kill my son?"

Surprised, the prophet asked if he were really to blame. "Yes indeed," she replied, "you are to blame. Before you came, I was considered a righteous woman compared to all the idolaters living in this place. But now that you live here, I seem wicked in comparison to you, a holy man. That is why Hashem punished me by taking my son."

These moving words coming from a broken heart distressed the prophet deeply. The widow had been so good to him; he did not want her to suffer. Without saying a word, he took the child from her arms and brought him up to an attic room. There he laid him out on the bed and began praying to Hashem, "Master of the universe, do not harm this good woman because of me. She is righteous and charitable. Give me the key of *techiyas hameisim*, so that I can revive her only son and restore him to her."

Hashem said to Eliyahu, "I cannot give you the key that you requested. This would leave me with only one key, the key to conception. Then everyone would say that you are mightier than I, possessing two keys—of rain and resurrection—while I have only one! If you really wish to have the key to *techiyas hameisim*, you must return the key to the rains." Eliyahu immediately gave back his first key and received the key to *techiyas hameisim* in return.

Now possessing this special power, Eliyahu placed himself on top of the lad. He put his mouth on the child's mouth, his eyes upon the lad's eyes, his hands and feet above the dead boy's limbs. Then he cried out, "Hashem, my G-d! Restore the soul of this child to his body." Hashem heard Eliyahu's prayer and returned the soul to the body. The boy stirred and awoke. Eliyahu got up and brought him back to his mother and said, "Here, you see that he lives."

With tears streaming down her cheeks, she thanked him. "Now I know that you are, indeed, a man of G-d, and G-d's word which you speak is truth." When this lad grew up, he also became a prophet. He was the famous Yonah (Hanavi).

3

ELIYAHU AND OVADYA

Queen Izevel, the wicked non-Jewish wife of King Achav, had ordered her servants to kill off all the true prophets of Hashem. Many were, indeed, slain by the cruel king and queen. But one hundred prophets remained alive, thanks to Ovadya, an important figure at the royal palace. Ovadya was a G-d-fearing man, who had hidden these hundred men away, safe from the arm of Izevel, fifty in one cave and another fifty in another. He brought them food and water each day, at great personal risk and trouble. He was generously rewarded for his devotion.

Ovadya was also well-liked by the king. As the famine spread, bearing down heavily upon the land, the king once asked Ovadya to join him in searching for a source of water. "Perhaps we will find some dried hay for our animals so that they won't die," the king suggested hopefully. "Perhaps through the animals, we will also be saved, for they are not judged like we humans are. They subsist entirely upon the mercy of Hashem. If there is still a supply of food and water for them, we will be able to stay alive by sharing it." King Achav and Ovadya then went their separate ways, both in search of some food or water.

While they were searching, Hashem said to the prophet Eliyahu, "I have brought famine upon My people for three years. The time has now come for you to go to Achav and inform him of the coming rains. I have decided to bring rain."

On his way to the king's palace, the prophet met Ovadya. He told him to return to Achav and inform him that Eliyahu was on his way to meet him. Ovadya knew how hard and long the king had been looking for Eliyahu and was now afraid of being made a fool. "You tell me to return to my master and inform him that you are on your way to him. But what if you suddenly disappear? What if the wind suddenly wafts you away? The king will kill me for deceiving him. Don't you know what Izevel did to all the *neviim*? She commanded that they all be wiped out! I succeeded in concealing one hundred of them in two caves among the mountains. I am the only one who knows where they are hidden. I bring them food and water each day. If I die, they will also die," Ovadya explained humbly. Eliyahu calmed him, assuring him that he would follow right after and bear out his words. Ovadya then agreed to go to the king and tell him that Eliyahu was coming to see him on a mission from Hashem.

When the king heard that he was finally to see the man whom he had been seeking high and low, he hurried forward to intercept him. When he saw him approaching, he called out, "Is that you, the despoiler of Israel? The destroyer of the nation! It is your fault that there is no rain. Have you no pity for the people and the animals suffering because of the famine, and all because of you?"

"Do not call me a 'despoiler of Israel'!" the *navi* hurried to reply. "You are the one who is killing off our people. You and your wicked forefathers are guilty, with your idolatry and wickedness. You forced me to call for this famine and drought. And now, go and gather all the people. I wish to show you who is the real and mighty G-d. He will send us rain, for He is a merciful G-d, ready to forgive even sinners like yourself."

4

ELIYAHU ON MOUNT CARMEL

One of the great miracles that Eliyahu performed before all of Israel took place on Mount Carmel. In order to prove to the people once and for all who was truly the Creator, the all-powerful force in the world, he said to Achav, "I know that you and your men worship idols. You claim that they are the powers in this world. Come, let us see now who is the Almighty G-d. Gather all of the priests of the Baal on Mount Carmel. We will build two altars there and take twin calves. I will sacrifice one upon the altar which I will build, while the priests of Baal shall sacrifice the second calf on the altar which they shall build. Whichever 'god' sends his fire to consume the sacrifice on the altar is to be publicly recognized as the Almighty."

This suggestion pleased the king. He felt certain that his god, the Baal, which his wife had introduced into the country, could send fire down from heaven. Later, at home, King Achav told his friend Chiel what Eliyahu had suggested. Chiel encouraged the king, "Don't worry, Your Majesty. Just leave everything up to me. You will see that everything will turn out just fine. We will outsmart Eliyahu. We will build a hollow altar in which I will hide, holding a vessel full of burning coals. As soon as our priests begin shouting for the Baal to send fire, I will sprinkle my coals upon the altar from underneath, and lo! The wood under the sacrifice will be ignited, burning the animal above it!"

"What an excellent idea!" the king congratulated Chiel and began planning the coming event. He sent his proclamation throughout all the cities of the land. "Everyone is to gather at Mount Carmel. Do not fail to come!" The people heard and obeyed, thronging in masses to witness the great spectacle that was to take place on Mount Carmel. They came to see who, in truth, was G-d.

Identical twin calves were brought before the king and Eliyahu. Lots were thrown to see which would be sacrificed to Hashem and which (*lehavdil*) to the Baal. The calf singled out for Hashem ran forward to Eliyahu, but the second animal refused to budge. All of the four hundred and fifty prophets of the Baal tried to push the calf, but it would not move. Eliyahu understood why it refused to budge. He whispered in its ear, "Go, because that is how the lots have fallen." It still would not move. To the surprise of all those gathered, it opened its mouth and began talking, "My brother and I were born of the same mother. We grew up together, grazed in the same pasture, ate from the same trough. Why should my brother have the privilege of sanctifying Hashem's name by being sacrificed on Eliyahu's altar, while I must be sacrificed to a false god made by man? My brother will gladden Hashem and glorify His Name, while I will only anger my Creator. I refuse to go."

Eliyahu realized the justice of these arguments and reassured the poor animal. "Do not say that you will not sanctify the Name of Hashem. The opposite is true. If you refuse to go with the priests of the Baal, you will be providing them will all kinds of arguments and excuses and nothing will be proved. But if you do agree to go with them, all will see the worthlessness of the Baal. Thus Hashem's Name will truly be sanctified and glorified in public!" The calf still would not move until Eliyahu himself led it to the priests of the Baal, walking by its side all the way. The poor beast advanced humbly towards its fate.

Eliyahu stood opposite the masses of people who had gathered from all corners of the land and declared aloud, "Listen to me, O Children of Israel! How much longer will you go limping between two opinions without making your final choice? When will you decide who is the true G-d? If it is Hashem, then follow Him and observe His command-ments. If you say that the Baal created the world, then worship him." Stunned by these words, the Jews stood there trans-fixed. They still could not decide. Eliyahu continued, "You know that only I have remained of all the true prophets of Hashem. Opposite me stand four hundred and fifty prophets of the Baal. You see here two calves, both of which we will sacrifice. One of them will be sacrificed by the prophets of the Baal, the other, I will offer up to the G-d of Israel. The test is to see which sacrifice will be accepted. Upon one sacrifice will a heavenly fire descend, proving once and for all who is the true G-d."

The people nodded in agreement and replied unanimous-ly, "Fine! That will be the final proof and will show us whom we should worship and serve."

The prophets of the Baal were first. Eliyahu said to them,

"Because you are the majority, you should have the first chance." The prophets of the Baal approached the hollow altar which they had built, arranged logs upon it, slaughtered their calf and placed it upon their altar. Then they all stood around, shouting, "Baal, answer us! Baal, answer us!" When he heard their shouts, Chiel, who was concealed within the altar, stretched out his hands to the burning coals. He was going to ignite the logs from underneath to give the impression to all the people that a miraculous fire had suddenly come down to consume the sacrifice. But just at that moment, a poisonous snake bit him, and he died. No one except the king had known about this deception; and he now stood there, disappointed and enraged that his plot had been foiled. The prophets of the Baal continued to cry out to their god to answer them, but all in vain. Nothing happened. The prophets began crying out to all the other gods that they knew of. They jumped about the altar in crazed frenzy, shouting and screaming; they tried all their magic, but nothing helped. There was no sign from heaven. At this time Hashem silenced the entire world. Not a bird or beast made a sound. All that could be heard were the desperate shouts of the false prophets, pleading, "Baal! Answer us!" Finally, they fell down in exhaustion, thoroughly ashamed and frustrated at their disgrace. In their stupor, they began attacking one another with their swords.

It took a long while for Eliyahu to quiet them down. When all was quiet, he turned to the people and said, "Gather close and watch as I offer my sacrifice before Hashem." It was already late in the afternoon, and Eliyahu wished to show Hashem's greatness while it was still daylight. He therefore turned to the sun and said, "Sun! Sun! You stopped traveling in your orbit in the time of Yehoshua so that he could defeat his enemies before the Sabbath. Stand still once again so that I may sanctify Hashem's Name before this huge congregation. Stand still again, not for the sake of Yehoshua or for the sake of the Jews, but purely for the sake of Hashem. Let all of Israel see that Hashem, and only Hashem, is the true G-d."

The sun obeyed Eliyahu and stopped traveling across the sky. Meanwhile, Eliyahu began his preparations. He first built an altar of twelve stones to symbolize the twelve tribes of Israel. He laid branches across the top, then dug a trench all around it. He then called Elisha, his disciple, and told him to fill up a pail with water and pour it over his hands. When Elisha poured the water, Eliyahu's fingers suddenly turned into ten fountains spouting water. The water continued to flow until the entire trench around the altar was filled with water. After placing the slaughtered calf upon his altar, Eliyahu prayed to Hashem, "Answer me, O Hashem! Answer me! Send down Your holy fire from heaven lest the prophets of the Baal claim that You are no more capable of sending down fire than was their god, the Baal. In Your abundant kindness, do what I have asked, Hashem, so that my words be not empty promises and boasts. For if the Jews do not see Your greatness and power now, they will never listen to me when I come to announce the final redemption."

Hashem heeded Eliyahu's prayer and in full view of all the people gathered, sent a fire down from heaven which burned up Eliyahu's sacrifice and even dried up all the water in the trench. The people were so overwhelmed that they fell upon their faces and cried aloud, "Hashem is the true G-d! "Hashem is the true G-d!"

Taking advantage of the heavenly good will at this auspicious moment, Eliyahu also asked Hashem to send blessed rains. "Please, Hashem! Send rain down for Your children! And even if we are not worthy of it, do it for the sake of the *bris* which the sons of Avraham, your loyal servant, still observe." As he was praying, it suddenly began raining heavily. The rain penetrated into the earth that had been parched for three years. The earth drank thirstily and was satisfied.

5

MOUNT CARMEL

Why was Mount Carmel chosen from among all other mountains as the site for this miraculous happening?

When Hashem was about to give the Torah to His people, He looked for the proper site for this monumental event. All the mountains fought among themselves for the great privilege. They all rushed to the desert, for they knew the Torah would be given in the desert, a place belonging to no one. Thus, anyone or any nation who desired to receive the Torah and accept its way of life could feel free to do so. They did not have to worry about anyone claiming that they had no right to approach the site of the Revelation.

And so, all the mountains congregated in the desert began quarreling. "Go back to where you came from!" shouted Mount Tavor to Mount Carmel."No one invited you here!"

Refusing, Mount Carmel countered, "You go back to your place. I am worthy of the Divine Presence." To this, Mount Tavor said, "But I am higher than you! I am so high that the waters of the Flood never even reached my neck! I am the worthier one!" Now Mount Hermon butted in, "Who are you to quarrel over the privilege of receiving the Torah? Surely the Torah will be given on me. It befits only me. How do you think the Jews were able to cross the Red Sea? I came to the sea bed and they walked upon my back."

In the midst of all this arguing, a heavenly voice rang out, "Why are you getting so excited? Why are you disputing? You have been disqualified because of your very quarreling! None of you will enjoy the privilege that you are seeking. Hashem will not give the Torah upon any of you! He will give it on one mountain that is humble and unassuming, Mount Sinai, the mountain upon which no idolatry was ever practiced. This mountain is sacred. Man's hand has not yet defiled it. This mountain is actually part of Mount Moriah upon which Avraham brought up Yitzchak to be sacrificed. Upon this mountain Hashem said, 'Since Yitzchak was bound up here for a sacrifice, it is only fitting that the Torah be given to his descendants upon this very mountain.' Some day Mount Sinai will return to its original site, as the prophet Yeshayahu has predicted, 'The mountain of Hashem's House shall be established on the top of the mountains.' That is Mount Moriah upon which the Beis Hamikdash was, and once again will be, built."

Ashamed and disappointed, the mountains returned to their separate places, saying to Hashem, "Do we not deserve some reward for our eagerness that your Torah be given upon us?" Hashem admitted, "Do not be grieved, for you will rewarded for your efforts. I will bring deliverance to Israel upon Mount Tavor during the time of Devorah and perform great miracles on Mount Carmel during the time of Eliyahu when My Name will be sanctified before all of Israel."

6

Reward for the Love of Torah

Of all the kings of Israel, Achav was the most wicked and most sinful. People used to say, "The light sins of Achav are comparable to the weighty sins of Yeravam ben Nevat." Although Achav worshipped all the gods of that time, he nevertheless loved the Torah and spent much time studying it. The king also favored Torah scholars, honored them and even supported them with his own money so that they might continue to study without having to worry about a livelihood. Hashem rewarded him for this with a victory over his enemy, Ben Haddad, King of Aram.

Ben Haddad had gathered in his army and asked thirty-two kings to join him in fighting against the Jews. His huge army encamped in the city of Shomron and prepared for the attack. To provoke Achav to start the war, Ben Haddad sent messengers to him with the following declaration, "You must give me all of your gold and silver. Your property is mine. And your most able wives and sons must also be delivered to me. Not only that, you must give me the Torah scroll which I have heard you cherish so. If you refuse, I will be forced to declare war upon you, and you will surely regret it. I have mustered a huge combined force of my allies who have large armies, strong arms, mighty horses and horsemen. If you do not hand over all that I have requested, we will storm through your country, kill you and your supporters and conquer your land." This brazen message frightened the king. How could he possibly stand up to a combined army like that?

Achav told his elderly advisors what the King of Aram had threatened and asked them what to do. They replied, "Your Majesty! If you wish to appease him with gold and silver, with your wives and children, go ahead and do so. Just one thing, do not give that wicked man our holy Torah! It is too precious to us even if we worship false gods and do not obey all that is written in it." The king agreed with their advice and bravely replied to the messengers, "I would willingly give you all that you have demanded. But I refuse to give up our most valuable treasure, the Torah."

Achav's daring reply angered Ben Haddad. He sent a second warning with other messengers, "Since you have refused my request, I am attacking your country. My soldiers will invade your soil and will be so numerous that there will be no room for them all to stand!" Achav was not frightened by these threats any more and courageously told them not to boast before they carried them out. "Who knows if you will really succeed after all? Save your victory song for after the war!"

Achav's message reached Ben Haddad as he was celebrating the victory that he was certain would be his. And before he even had time to declare war, he was attacked by Achav's troops in a surprise offensive. The drunken king did not have his wits about him and was defeated.

But he would not admit his defeat yet. He said, "I fought

the Jews upon the mountains. Hashem is G-d of the mountains. Let us see how He fights us on the plains and in the valleys!" After issuing his proud challenge, he prepared for the next battle.

Meanwhile the prophet Michayhu came to Achav with a message from Hashem, "Thus says Hashem: Go muster your forces and attack Ben Haddad once more. Because you protected the Torah and refused to surrender it to the tainted hands of the enemy, I will deliver this enemy into your power. And because the king of Aram boasted that I am only a G-d of the mountains, I will show him and his army that I can subdue him wherever they stand. I will show them all that I am Hashem, the Almighty, and that there is no power to compare with Mine. And when Ben Haddad is captured, make sure that you show him no pity. Do not let him remain alive, even if he pleads and begs for his life. I have warned you! If you let him live, I will claim your own life instead!"

Confident of victory, Achav went forth against the king of Aram and defeated him this time as well. When the king saw his end before him, he quickly donned sackcloth and, together with his ranking ministers, came on bended knee before Achav to beg for his life. He promised to return to Achav all the cities which his father had once seized from Achav's father, Amri. Achav's great victory made him forget the prophet's threat, and he did not kill Ben Haddad as Hashem had commanded.

Hashem then sent His prophet Michayhu once again, with the following message, "Because you did not obey My command to kill Ben Haddad when he was in your power, you deserve to be punished. But since you were ready to sacrifice yourself for My Torah, you will be rewarded with an additional twenty-two years on the throne, corresponding to the twenty-two letters of the *aleph-beis* with which the Torah is written."

7

THE STOLEN VINEYARDS

Navos the Yizraelite owned a vineyard next to the property of the king. The king coveted this particular vineyard since he had a grand plan of creating a beautiful park surrounding the palace.

Navos was a righteous person. He possessed a lovely voice and used to entertain and inspire the Jews who gathered in Jerusalem on the three Festivals. People did not stop praising his singing, and many people made the pilgrimage to Jerusalem just to hear him. Hashem had blessed him with this gift so that he could use it to praise Him and to draw more and more people to the Beis Hamikdash. But all this praise went to Navos' head and made him boastful. He told himself, "Next Festival I will not go to Jerusalem. Let's see if I am missed."

Navos should not have thought so highly of himself. His gift was from Hashem; its purpose was to glorify Him. Since he misused it, he was punished. Indeed, Achav killed him.

The king did not wish to take Navos' vineyard without the owner's permission. He therefore sent some of his men with an offer for Navos. "The king will give you a better vineyard or, if you prefer, will pay you what it is worth." But Navos refused to sell his property. "It was handed down to me by my fathers. It is a family heritage from generations back." Navos' refusal angered the king. He was so upset that his wife, Izevel, could not help noticing his gloom that evening. She asked him why he was so sad, and he told her what had happened.

"Do not disturb yourself on his account," she soothed him. "I will get his vineyard for you. Is it fitting that a king should bow to the will of his subject? Leave this all up to me."

That very day, Izevel wrote to the Elders commanding them to seize Navos the Yizraelite and bring against him two false witnesses who would testify that he had committed treason and therefore should be put to death. She signed the order with the king's own seal. Armed with this document, the judges had Navos seized. He was then falsely accused and executed.

Feeling very pleased, Achav went down to visit the vineyard which became his upon the death of its owner. He felt not even a twinge of guilt over his terrible deed. As he was walking around, inspecting the grounds, he was suddenly confronted by Eliyahu Hanavi who had been sent by Hashem to warn him of his imminent death. He admonished him, "What have you done? Shall you murder and inherit as well? Are you not ashamed? You commanded an innocent man to be killed merely for having refused to sell you his only vineyard, an inheritance from his forefathers. Since you did this evil thing, your end shall be bitter indeed. You shall die in shame; your blood will be drunk by dogs in the place where they licked Navos' blood. Your wife Izevel will also be severely punished. The dogs will eat her flesh as well, after she has died through terrible suffering. Hashem has watched your sins long enough. He has had enough of your inciting the people to sin. He will take your kingdom away from you and wipe out your entire family. No trace will remain of them. Your relatives who die in the city will be eaten by dogs, while those who die in the field will be the prey of fowl." The prophet's words terrified the king. He tore his clothing, put on sackcloth, placed ashes on his head and began to fast. He wanted to repent for all of his sins.

King Yehoshafat of Judah also heard about the terrible death in store for Achav. He quickly came to visit so that he might offer his good advice. "Why must you be so sad?" he asked. "Don't you know that Hashem does not seek the death of the wicked? He prefers that they repent and live! Hashem waits for the *teshuvah* of sinners. You can still repent. Wait and see if Hashem does not accept your *teshuvah*."

Achav listened to Yehoshafat and began to repent. He fasted and wept. He begged Yehoshafat to give him forty lashes, three times a day. And throughout, he prayed to Hashem for mercy, day and night, until Hashem finally accepted his *teshuvah* and decreed that the throne would not be taken away from him. The dreadful prophecy would not come to pass in his lifetime. Hashem then said to Eliyahu Hanavi, "Do you see the wonderful gift that I have given to the world? A person may sin and may anger Me, but when he repents and shows genuine regret over his deeds, I accept his *teshuvah* and forgive him."

8

ACHAV'S BITTER END

The Jews lived upon their land in peace and comfort for the next three years. In the third year, Yehoshafat came to Achav, King of Judah, and Achav begged him to be his ally against Aram. A good friend of Achav's, Yehoshafat did not disappoint him. "I will surely join you. My people are your people. My horses are your horses. I, too, am at your service." They prepared for battle.

Before setting out, Achav gathered four hundred prophets of the Baal and asked them if he would be successful or not. They replied, "Go, for Hashem has delivered them into your hands." They used Hashem's Name so that Yehoshafat, a G-d-fearing king who did not worship idols, would think that they were true prophets. Still, the king of Judah did not believe them.

"I have never heard even two prophets using the same style of speech. How can it be that four hundred men use the very same words?" he thought. He asked if there was another prophet whom they could consult.

Achav replied, "I do know one other prophet, but I don't like to hear what he says, for he is always scolding and rebuking me. He is Michayhu ben Yimla. Indeed, I hate him, for he is always predicting evil things."

"Call him, nevertheless," Yehoshafat responded. "I would like to hear what he has to say."

Achav's servants went in search of the prophet Michayhu. Before they had returned, a prophet of the Baal, Tzidkiyahu ben Kenaana, came before the king and presented him with a pair of iron horns. "With these horns will you gore Aram. Have no fear. You will surely be victorious over your enemy. Hashem has already delivered him into your hands." At this, the other prophets of the Baal cheered joyfully and encouraged the king to go forth.

While they were still shouting and cheering, injecting enthusiasm into the large crowd that had gathered, the prophet of Hashem appeared. When the king asked him if he should go to fight Aram, Michayhu replied, "You have asked me, Your Majesty, and I will answer. You have sworn me to tell only the truth. Therefore, listen carefully. I see all of Israel being dispersed among the hills like a sheep without a shepherd. If you go out to this war you will surely be defeated. You will not return in peace. Know that it has been decreed in heaven that you shall fight against Aram. Hashem sat upon His heavenly throne and held council, His ministering angels standing to His left and right. He asked them, 'Who will be the one to coax Achav into fighting this war in which he will die?' The spirit of Navos the Yizraelite, who was so brutally killed by Izevel, Achav's wife, volunteered to get the prophets of the Baal to tempt Achav to wage the war from which he would not come back alive."

These words shocked both kings. Yehoshafat, who believed in Hashem and in what the prophet had predicted, hesitated for a moment, but rallied. It was a decree from heaven that he fight against Aram, and so he must go. Achav, the sinner, became inflamed and said, "Did I not tell you that this prophet is always predicting gloom and doom? I refuse to believe what he says." Tzidkiyahu ben Kenaana, the false prophet, backed up the king. He walked over to Michayhu and slapped him across the face even as Achav was ordering his servants to seize Michayhu. "Put him in jail and let him remain imprisoned until I return home safely and peaceful-ly!" the king shouted, not believing that he would really die.

Achav's end was a bitter one. He was killed by an arrow that miraculously penetrated his armor and entered his heart. This was one of the few times that Hashem made a relatively soft substance (the arrow) overcome something much harder than itself (the armor). Achav died courageously. He was struck while riding in a chariot, but did not reveal this even to his driver. He did not want to frighten his soldiers with the sight of their king dying. He simply told the driver to take him back home, and, with his remaining strength, stood up all the way lest anyone flee in panic on seeing that he had been injured. Towards evening, when he finally reached the pal-ace, he collapsed and died. But the news of his death spread rapidly in the camp, and this caused the very flight he had tried to prevent, leaving the Arameans exulting in victory.

Achav was given a royal burial in Shomron. His coffin was preceded by thirty-six thousand men, and he was eulo-gized with great honor. When the war was finally over, the king's bloody chariot was washed in the pool of Shomron. Dogs lapped up this water, thus fulfilling Eliyahu's prophecy to Achav in the vineyard of Navos.

Achav's soul ascended to heaven and stood fearfully before the Throne of Judgment. The Heavenly Court could not decide what to do with him. Should he go to Gan Eden for having repented or go to Gehinnom for having sinned so much? Suddenly, the spirit of Navos the Yizraelite, who had been murdered, appeared and tipped the scale. He was sentenced to Gehinnom. The wicked king's soul was taken to the fifth level of lower Gehinnom where the angel Oniel reigns. But because of Hashem's great mercy, Achav was spared torture. He is the only soul among ten thousand sinners there who is not punished every single day. But even though Hashem took pity on him and spared him the suffering of Gehinnom, still he will never be allowed to enter Gan Eden, for he was the most wicked of all kings. He sinned and deliberately caused his people to sin along with him. His is therefore one of the most severe punishments Hashem ever meted out to a Jew.

9

Eliyahu, Prophet of Hashem

Eliyahu was unique among our nation's prophets. Actually, he was created first as an angel. When Hashem was about to create man, He gathered His angels and told them, "Let us make a man in Our likeness and Our form." The angels were opposed to this. "Hashem, our Master," they said, "why must You create such a being who will only anger and disobey You?" Eliyahu Hanavi, who was then an angel, disagreed with them. "Master of the universe! If it pleases You to create man, I am willing to descend to earth and to serve mankind." This pleased Hashem. He promised to send Eliyahu down to earth when the proper time came.

This time came during the reign of the wicked Achav, who caused all of Israel to sin. Hashem summoned Eliyahu and told him, "Go now, and strengthen the faith in Me among My people." Eliyahu lived among the Jewish people during the era of Achav and of his son, Achazya. He was faced with idols, which had been set up throughout the land by the wicked kings. Eliyahu tried to show the people the worthlessness of these idols and the greatness of the Creator. Indeed, Eliyahu publicized Hashem's greatness through the wonders of miracles, and thereby succeeded in restoring many to the faith of their fathers. When the time came for Eliyahu to return to heaven, Hashem said, "Since you succeeded in sanctifying My Name among My children who had deserted Me, I am appointing you as My people's guardian. Through you, My Name will always be sanctified from now on."

Eliyahu enjoyed divine revelation on a very high level. When he was fleeing from Izevel, who wished to kill him for having ordered the death of four hundred and fifty prophets of the Baal, Eliyahu reached Mount Chorev. He entered a secluded cave and suddenly heard the voice of Hashem speaking to him. On this occasion, Hashem showed Eliyahu all that would happen to each person in history, from his birth until after his death.

"Go outside and stand before Hashem on the mountain," Eliyahu heard the voice saying to him. And then suddenly he heard a mighty wind smashing boulders and destroying mountains. Then there was an earthquake followed by a glowing fire. Hashem did not appear with the wind, the earthquake or the fire. At last, all that remained was a faint whisper, and Hashem's voice could be heard.

Through the wind, the earthquake, the fire and the stillness, Hashem had shown Eliyahu the four worlds which a person must pass through from the day of his birth until his soul returns to its source in heaven. The great wind represents this world, which is like a passing wind. The earthquake is the day of death which seizes a person's body and shakes it up as the soul is about to leave. The fire is that of Gehinnom which the soul must pass through to be purified if its many sins outweigh its *mitzvos*. And finally, the faint voice is the Presence of Hashem, which will remain all alone in the world at the end of time, as it is written, "and Hashem alone will remain exalted and alone on that day."

Eliyahu continued to circulate among the people for three years after this revelation. He prophesied, rebuked them and helped them repent until his time came to return to heaven. After Eliyahu anointed Elisha as his successor, the latter did not leave him for a moment. Elisha served his master day and night and learned Torah from him. On the day that Eliyahu was supposed to ascend to heaven, he tried to slip away from Elisha. So modest and humble was he that he did not want anyone to see that marvelous sight. But Elisha knew through divine inspiration that his master was to leave him and therefore refused to budge from his side. The two walked together until they reached the Jordan. Here, Eliyahu removed his cloak and struck the water with it. The river split and the two crossed over on dry land.

When the Angel of Death learned that Eliyahu was to rise to heaven without dying first like all other men, he appeared before Hashem and complained, "Master of the universe, did You not entrust me with the souls of all mankind? Am I not charged with reclaiming them when the time comes? Why may I not take Eliyahu's soul as well? If I am not allowed to take it, then other men will also refuse to give me their souls. My office will become meaningless!"

Hashem listened to his plea and said, "Eliyahu Hanavi is different from other people. He is stronger even than you and has the power to destroy you. I created heaven and earth so that Eliyahu might descend to earth and one day return to heaven. But if you still want to try your luck, go down and see if you can overcome him!" The Angel of Death descended to earth and stood before Eliyahu. The latter grabbed hold of him, threw him to the ground and stood firmly on top of him, almost killing the Angel of Death. But Hashem's voice rang out and said, "Leave him be. Do not harm him. Tie him up so that he does not harm you. Then come up to heaven."

Eliyahu looked up and saw a fiery chariot with horses of fire approaching him. Aware that his time had come, he turned to Elisha and said, "I must leave you now. Make one last request, and I will grant it." Trembling and full of emotion, Elisha asked to have double the measure of prophecy that Eliyahu enjoyed. "That is a truly difficult request," Eliyahu admitted. "I can only give you what I had, not more. But if you succeed in seeing me taken up to heaven, this will be your sign that Hashem has granted your wish."

They were still talking when a brilliant and marvelous light filled the sky. Since they were preoccupied with studying Torah, the angel sent to fetch Eliyahu would not approach. But when they stopped for a minute to look at the wondrous scene, the angel quickly seized Eliyahu and put him into the chariot. It then rose upward in a storm of wind. Elisha saw it all. He was so overcome with emotion that he cried out, "My father! My father! The chariot of Israel and its horsemen!" He tore his clothes in pain and never sewed them up again.

Eliyahu was given a hero's welcome in heaven. He was assigned a place at the crossroads of heaven to show *tzaddikim* their place in Gan Eden. Every Friday afternoon, at sunset, Eliyahu goes to Gehinnom and removes the sinners from there. He brings them to Gan Eden where they can rejoice on *Shabbos*, free from the week's suffering. But right after *Shabbos*, he must return them to their places. When a person's sin is expiated, and he no longer needs to be purified in the fires of Gehinnom, it is Eliyahu who comes to fetch him and lead him to his place in Gan Eden. When he is not busy doing this, Eliyahu sits in heaven and records all the deeds of mankind. Nothing is hidden from him. He is ever ready for the command to go down and tell the Jewish people that the time of redemption, the *geulah*, has come.

10

Eliyahu Rescues the Jewish People

Throughout his lifetime, Eliyahu labored to make the Jews repent. And he tried to help anyone in need. Only once, when many were seeking to kill him at Izevel's command, did his strong spirit break, and he spoke against his people.

It happened when Hashem appeared to him on Mount Chorev. Hashem asked him what he was doing there. He replied, "I am running away from Jews who wish to kill me. I am angry at Your Jewish people for having forsaken Your Torah, demolished Your altars and killed all of Your prophets." These words displeased Hashem. No matter how much Jews sin, they still remain Hashem's children, and He still loves them. "Why do you speak against My people?" He asked. "Is it your Torah that they have abandoned, your altars which they have destroyed? If they have forgotten My *bris* and killed My prophets, I still forgive them, for I love them so much. If you cannot bear them, go back and anoint Elisha ben Shafat from Avel Mechola as a prophet in your place. If you think that they are wicked, go to Damascus and see how the non-Jews behave! There are three hundred and sixty-five different types of idols there, all of which they worship daily. Yet, do I not allow the sun to shine for them? Do I not give them moonlight? Follow My example. Learn to see the good, and be an advocate for My people!"

From that time on, Eliyahu spoke only good about the Jews. Even after he ascended to heaven, he did not forget his people and continued to care for them. And he still does! Eliyahu reveals himself to the wholly righteous in different guises: sometimes as a beggar, sometimes as a rider mounted on a mighty horse, sometimes as an important minister in the court of some gentile king and sometimes even as an Arab. With four flutters of his wings, Eliyahu can fly from one end of the world to the other without ever tiring from doing good and showing mercy to those who deserve it.

Eliyahu frequently appears to Torah scholars. He is the connection, the ambassador between the *yeshivah shel maalah* and the earthly *yeshivah*. He reveals the secrets of the Torah to both sages and *tzaddikim*. Many miracles have been performed by him. He has rescued the poor and the sick and has enabled the barren to bear children. Sometimes, when he cannot help a Jew who is suffering, he at least comforts and encourages him to pray to Hashem for help.

11

ELIYAHU'S ROLE IN THE FUTURE

In the time of *Mashiach*, Eliyahu Hanavi will bring the Jews the good tidings of redemption, as it is written, "Behold I am sending Eliyahu Hanavi to you before Hashem's great and fearful day." Before *Mashiach* comes, Eliyahu will come to the people and get them to repent. He will explain all that is difficult in the Torah and will reveal all of its secrets so that the Torah will be altogether clear to everyone, and all of Jewry will study it with joy. Eliyahu will not only repair the relations between the Jews and their heavenly Father, but will bring peace and love between man and wife, and between man and his fellow.

Then, when the people are truly worthy and ready for *Mashiach*, Eliyahu will climb a high mountain and cry out, "Hills of Israel, how long shall you remain desolate? The time of the redemption has come. Peace will reign in the world." The next day Eliyahu will return and exclaim, "Goodness has come to the world!" And on the third day he will declare, "Salvation has come to the world!" At this point, the angel Michael will blow upon a mighty *shofar*, and the *Mashiach* will be sent down from heaven to bring all the Jews to Eretz Yisrael from the ends of the earth.

THE PERIOD OF THE KINGS

After all the people have been gathered from their lands of exile, *Mashiach* will begin performing wonders and miracles before all so that they will truly believe that the end of their suffering and dispersion has finally come. He will then tell Eliyahu to blow one mighty blast upon his *shofar*. Suddenly an brilliant light will shine, the light from the first week of Creation, hidden until then. At the sound of a second blast from Eliyahu's *shofar*, all the dead will rise up and come to Eretz Yisrael. At the third blast, the glory of Hashem will be revealed to all of Jewry, and all will bask in the splendor of the Divine Presence. With the fourth blast of the *shofar*, all the mountains and hills will collapse into valleys. The entire land will be leveled out, and the Beis Hamikdash will be re-established in all its glory. Then shall Eliyahu sit at the right of *Mashiach*, David's descendant, as one of the eight princes who are foremost in his kingdom.

12

ELISHA THE PROPHET

Elisha ben Shafat, disciple and faithful attendant of Eliyahu, was one of Jewry's greatest prophets. After Eliyahu's ascent to heaven, Elisha became the people's prophet and leader. He led his people for sixty years, guiding, prophesying and performing miracles for them.

Elisha was rewarded with a degree of prophecy which no one before him had enjoyed, except for Moshe Rabbeinu, the father of all prophets. Since he selflessly left behind his property and his home to serve Eliyahu with utter devotion, Hashem rewarded him generously with a measure of prophecy double that which his master had possessed. This is what Elisha had asked of Eliyahu before the latter had risen up to heaven in the fiery chariot. Eliyahu had only been able to promise that "if you see me being taken away, you will know that your wish has been fulfilled." And the wish was indeed fulfilled. Eliyahu performed eight great miracles while Elisha performed twice that number.

13

ELISHA AND THE STUDENT PROPHETS

Weeping and mournful, Elisha watched his revered master ascending to heaven. When he realized that Eliyahu would not return, he started back for the place from which they had come. When he reached the Jordan, he struck it with the cloak that Eliyahu had removed. The waters split, just as they had for Eliyahu, and he was able to cross to the other side. The student prophets who had been standing on the banks of the river and had seen the waters split twice, exclaimed, "Elisha's feat is greater than Eliyahu's; the first time the river parted on account of their combined merit, while this time it parted for Elisha alone."

Elisha's tale of Eliyahu's ascent to heaven proved too amazing for them to believe. "This is not the first time that Eliyahu has disappeared," they said. "Many times the spirit of Hashem has wafted him aloft to some unknown place from which he has returned. Perhaps the same thing has happened now too. Let us go and search for him."

Elisha did not dare contradict them. "If I do not let them seek him out, they will say that I am being disrespectful to Eliyahu, and that because I wish to replace him, I told them that he would not return," Elisha thought. He said, "Do as you wish. Go and look for him."

For three days the student prophets searched for Eliyahu up mountains and down valleys, but they could not find him. When they returned, they finally admitted that Elisha must have told them the truth. They realized that Eliyahu would not return.

14

THE MIRACLE OF THE BITTER WATERS

Because their city's water was undrinkable, the people of Jericho came to Elisha and asked if he could help. The land was good, they said, but the water could not be drunk. Elisha was touched by their trouble. "Bring me a jar of salt," he said. He then took this jar and poured all the salt directly into the stream whose water the inhabitants used. The people of Jericho could not understand what the prophet was doing! Throwing salt into water that was already bitter? They regretted having come to him with their problem; he was only making matters much worse! But when Elisha commanded them to taste the water, they discovered, much to their amazement, that it was sweet! They understood that this was a great miracle, a cause for celebration.

The news of the miracle of the bitter waters soon spread throughout the city. Everyone rejoiced except for the boys who had earned their living by transporting good drinking water to the inhabitants. They had just lost an excellent livelihood. Embittered, they ran after Elisha and mocked him, saying, "Baldy! Baldy!" Compared to his teacher, Eliyahu, who had long, thick hair, Elisha seemed bald. Their disgusting behavior angered Elisha. Seeing through his divine vision that none of them would produce any decent Jews, for they were totally lacking in *mitzvos* and piety, he cursed them in the Name of Hashem. Suddenly, two bears burst out of the forest and devoured the boys. But there had been no forest before, nor had there been any bears in that vicinity! What had happened? Where had these come from? It was a double miracle.

But Hashem was displeased by Elisha's curse. He should have forgiven the boys even though they hurt him. Since he had not, Elisha was punished with a severe illness.

15

YEHOSHAFAT, KING OF JUDAH

Yehoshafat, son of Asa, King of Judah, was a G-d-fearing king. He carefully observed all of the *mitzvos* and showed great love for the Torah and its scholars. His faith was so strong that it did not even waver in times of trouble. When he and Achav went to battle against Aram and were being repelled, he lifted his eyes to heaven and begged for help. Hashem heard his prayers and spared him. Yehoshafat returned home safely.

Yehoshafat was immensely wealthy. He had won spoils of much gold and silver in a war against Ammon, treasures which had once belonged to his father. Besides these which he restored to his own treasury, he added other spoils. Despite his wealth, his power and his status as king, Yehoshafat remained simple and humble. He never raised his voice, always went into battle together with his troops and never enjoyed the special privileges coming to him as king.

Yehoram, King of Israel, once asked Yehoshafat to join him in battle against the Moabites who had rebelled against him and who had stopped paying taxes. "I am ready to join you," Yehoshafat said. "We will be allies. My horses are yours; my people are yours." The two kings then assembled a large army and went forth to attack Moav. The king of Edom joined them since he was subjugated to Yehoram and forced to do his bidding. The three kings marched for seven days through the desert but could not find any water. Men and horses thirsted for water. They could not go any further. Not knowing how to remedy the situation, the kings and army commanders began to despair. "We cannot help ourselves without help from above. Let us seek a prophet of Hashem and ask him what to do."

Yehoram was not too keen about this idea. He said, "Only Elisha is in these parts. But he always prophesies doom. I don't think we should go to him for help." The king of Judah, however, was not afraid of hearing the word of Hashem. He removed his kingly robes, put on the uniform of a simple soldier and was about to go in search of Elisha. "What have you done?" the two other kings asked him. "Why are you dressed like a common soldier?"

"I am going to seek the word of Hashem," Yehoshafat replied humbly. "Before Him there is no difference between a rich man and a beggar, a king and a commoner. Today I do not feel like a king. I am thirsty and exhausted. Why should I wear my splendid robes? Come along with me, and let us seek help from Hashem." These words penetrated deep into the hearts of the two other kings and full of hope, they went together to find Elisha.

When Elisha saw them approaching, he turned first to Yehoram and said, "What business do you have with me? Why have you come? Go to the prophets of your mother and your father. Perhaps they can save you. Why have you come to ask help from the G-d of Israel, Whom you have abandoned? If it were not for Yehoshafat, King of Judah, I would not bother to speak to you!"

Yehoram was shaken by such strong words and said, "Please, my master! Don't be angry with me now that we are in such distress!" The prophet's anger did not please Hashem. Indeed, in time of trouble, he should have contained his anger and spoken respectfully. In punishment, Hashem took away his spirit of prophecy.

Not knowing what to tell the kings, Elisha stood there, speechless. Finally, he spoke, "If you can bring someone who can play a musical instrument, perhaps the divine spirit will return to me." Some music was played and his spirit of prophecy did, indeed, return. Now he was able to tell them what to do. "Listen to the word of Hashem; behold His incomparable greatness and might! Do you see this wadi before you? It is all dried up. Behold, Hashem will make pits in it and will fill them with water. You will not feel a wind nor see rain. Still they will overflow with plentiful fresh water for you and your animals. Furthermore, your enemies, the Moabites, will fall before you, not because you deserve this, but so that you may know that there is no Force like Hashem." The words had hardly been uttered before the dry wadi began flowing with water. Men and animals drank thirstily and gratefully.

The Moabites saw the water flowing from afar. Knowing that no rain had fallen, they thought the water pits and streams were flowing with blood. "It must mean that the three kings had a falling-out and warred among themselves," they concluded, bursting into shouts of joy. "They have done our work for us by killing each other off. Now all we have to do is go and gather up the loot." They rushed forward towards the three kings and their armies, who had meanwhile refreshed themselves with the good water. The latter had no trouble subduing the Moabites who were totally unprepared. Their army was demolished, and the remaining soldiers fled homeward.

In accordance with Hashem's wishes, the prophet Elisha ordered the Jewish armies to pursue them and destroy the Moabite cities, to chop down all their trees, fill their water holes with stones and destroy every good field. Yehoshafat objected to chopping down fruit trees, as forbidden by the Torah, but Elisha overruled him in the Name of Hashem, "You are correct that it is not right to chop down fruit trees even if they belong to the enemy, but Moav is not the usual kind of enemy. That nation did not welcome you when you wished to pass through their country on your way to Eretz Yisrael. They are despised in the eyes of Hashem, and you need not have mercy on them or their property."

The Moabite king fled for his very life. When he reached his palace safely, he called a council of all his advisors and magicians and rebuked them, "Before I left, you promised me that I would be able to defeat any people I chose to make war on and conquer their land. What happened to your prediction?"

Full of fear, they explained, "That is what we promised, Your Majesty, because that is what we were told by our gods. What they said is true concerning every nation except for the Jews, who are special; they are invincible. Why? Because their forefather, Avraham, was a servant of G-d and in his old age was prepared to sacrifice the son born to him when he was one hundred years old!"

The king of Moav replied, "If the G-d of Israel pays such a bountiful reward to one who merely intended to fulfill a commandment but did not do so, how much more shall He reward a person who actually fulfills His commandment?" His mind was already made up. He took his eldest son, the crown prince and offered him up as a sacrifice upon the city wall!

This deed reminded Hashem of the idolatry that the Jews still practiced, and He grew angry. Hashem had been so good to the Jews, had not ceased performing miracles and wonders for them from the time they had left Egypt, and yet they had abandoned His Torah to pursue foolish idols. Hashem was almost ready to deliver them into Moav's hands, but in the merit of Ovadya's wife, a great *tzaddekess*, did not do so. He allowed the Jews to return to their homes, crowned with victory.

16

REWARD FOR THE RIGHTEOUS

The prophet Ovadya was extremely wealthy. And even though he was upright and G-d-fearing, King Achav respected him greatly and spared him when his own wife, Izevel, commanded that all the prophets of Hashem be exterminated. Indeed, Ovadya succeeded in saving one hundred prophets thanks to his connections with the king. He hid them in two caves among the mountains and supported them from his own pocket. He was rewarded for his great efforts and self-sacrifice with the gift of prophecy. Hashem declared: Let Ovadya, a *tzaddik*, who lived among those two sinners Achav and Izevel, yet did not learn from their wicked example, come and prophesy about Edom, the nation which stems from Eisav, who lived between two *tzaddikim* Yitzchak and Rivkah, yet did not learn from their pious example.

Even after Achav's death, when his son Yehoram ruled, the hundred true prophets were afraid to come out of hiding for fear of being killed, since Yehoram was also an idolater. And so Ovadya continued to support and feed them. When his money was all used up, he still did not abandon them but borrowed money at interest from King Yehoram so that he might continue to bring them food.

After Ovadya's death, his widow and two children remained penniless. To make their situation even worse, King
Yehoram sent his collectors to demand the money that Ovadya
owed them, with interest. They came with the following
message, "Your husband owed me much money. If you do not
return the entire sum at once, I will seize your two children
and take them as slaves." The widow wept and pleaded that
she did not have anything in the house, did not own any
property and had no way of returning the money. But the
king's messengers, cruel like their master, refused to listen.
The king had told them to bring back either the money or the
sons. They were about to take the lads away by force.

The widow rushed to the cemetery where her husband was
buried and cried, "O One who feared Hashem!" A voice
echoed forth in response, "There are four great men who
feared Hashem: Avraham, Yosef, Iyov and Ovadya. Whom
do you seek?"

"I wish to speak to the one of whom it was said, 'He was
exceedingly fearful of Hashem.'" Heaven then indicated
which grave was Ovadya's. She threw herself upon it and
wept broken-heartedly. "My master and husband, our children and I are in great danger! The king has ordered his
servants to seize them if I do not pay our debt to him. I am
penniless. What shall I do?" Miraculously, the woman heard
her husband's voice speaking.

"Take the little oil that is left in the house to Elisha and ask
him to bless it. Tell him that I did not borrow the money from
the king for my own glory or use, but for Hashem's sake, to
feed the hundred true prophets whom I concealed in caves. I
provided for all their needs. The light of their oil lamps did not

go out by day or by night, for I took care of them. Tell all this to Elisha, and ask him to repeat these words before Hashem."

Trusting in Hashem's help, the woman went to Elisha and said, "My husband died, leaving us penniless. Worse yet, we owe great sums to the king, who has commanded that my sons be seized if the loan is not repaid immediately. Please save us! You know how very G-d-fearing my husband was!" The prophet asked her what she still had at home. "Just a small jar with a little bit of oil."

"Then do what I am about to tell you. Go to your neighbors and borrow all kinds of vessels from them. Then go home and lock yourselves in and begin pouring oil from your small jar into all the borrowed vessels. You will see, Hashem will bless you and save you."

The woman hurried to do what the prophet had instructed. Meanwhile, Elisha prayed for her and her sons. After she had closed the door behind them, the woman began pouring the oil from her small jar. And miracle of miracles! The oil filled all of the jars she had, but still the little jar continued to flow. Looking around, she spotted some broken vessels and exclaimed, "Let He Who commanded the empty vessels to fill up, also command the broken vessels to become whole and hold the oil." And behold, that additional miracle also came to pass. New vessels stood in place of the old, broken ones. And still, the oil continued to flow until every vessel in the house held oil.

Joyfully, the widow went to Elisha to report that Hashem had saved them. She wished to give away part of the oil as *terumah* and *maaser*, but Elisha said that this was unnecessary. Since this oil came about miraculously, it was not subject to the *maaser* obligation. "You have nothing to fear from the king's servants either," he said. "They need not know where the money came from or how you were able to pay back your debts. Hashem will silence them just as He did the dogs in Egypt when the Jews left that land."

Elisha told the good woman to sell the oil, and she earned a fortune from the sale. She was able to pay back her entire debt and still have much left over for her and her children. And when she died, she left her two sons a large inheritance.

17

THE SHUNAMITE WOMAN

Elisha traveled the length and breadth of the country. Wherever he went, he spoke to the people and tried to get them to repent. Of the many miracles he performed, two of the greatest were for the Shunamite woman. She was the wife of the prophet Ido and the sister of Avishag, King David's concubine in his old age. She was a righteous and generous woman. Hers was an open house; whoever came was greatly honored. She spared no expense or effort in pleasing her guests.

When Elisha passed through Shunaim he also stopped at her house to eat and rest up. This became a regular practice. The woman did not know his identity, but she realized that he was no simple traveler. Whenever he sat at her table, no fly would buzz about; his sheets remained spotless and uncreased, as if no one had slept on them, and a heavenly aroma rose from them. "He must surely be a man of G-d," she told her husband. "Let us build a small attic room where he can be comfortable. We will furnish it with a bed, table, chair and lamp. It will be set aside for his personal use and privacy." Her husband thought this was a good idea, and the plan was soon carried out. The prophet made use of it whenever he visited that city.

Time passed, and Elisha felt obligated to repay the woman for her exceptional hospitality in some special way. "What do you lack?" he once asked the couple. "Is there anything I can ask for you from the king or from his military commander? You take such pains to make my stay pleasant and comfortable; I would like to do something for you in return."

"I do not lack anything," the wife replied. "I have everything I need."

But Gaichazi, Elisha's young attendant, was standing by and noted, "The woman does not have any children."

The prophet realized that a son would complete the woman's happiness and blessed her. "Next year at this time you will be hugging a son." Surprised and overcome with emotion, she begged him not to ridicule her. She and her husband were already old. How could they have a child? She begged him not to disappoint her.

A year passed, and the couple were indeed blessed with a son. They were overjoyed and raised him devotedly. But one day when the lad went with his father to the fields to harvest, he suddenly felt a terrible pain in his head. His father brought him home at once, but it was too late to do anything. The boy died in the arms of his weeping mother. The woman did not hesitate but carried him up to the attic and laid him on Elisha's bed. Then she saddled her donkey and rushed to Elisha. Her husband asked her in surprise why she was going to him since it was not *Rosh Chodesh* or *Shabbos*, times when they would see the prophet. She did not remain to answer, however, but rode swiftly on. She went directly to Mount Carmel where Elisha usually stayed.

Elisha saw her coming from afar and sent Gaichazi to

inquire after her health and her family's welfare. She did not reveal the reason for her visit to Gaichazi, but when she approached Elisha, she went forward and threw herself at his feet. Gaichazi was about to brush her away so that she would not touch the prophet, but Elisha told him to leave her be. "She is embittered," he explained, "but Hashem has not revealed to me what sort of tragedy has befallen her."

In a tear-choked voice, the woman began, "Why did you ever bless me with a son? It would have been better if I had never borne him altogether, than to have been blessed with a son after so many years, only to lose him soon after."

The woman's pain touched the prophet deeply. He said, "Everything that Hashem does in this world, He usually informs me of beforehand. But this time He has not told me a thing! I know nothing of the lad's death. Therefore I have reason to hope that he may still live!" He turned to Gaichazi and instructed him, "Go quickly to this woman's house. Take my staff and place it on the lad's face. Make sure that you do not speak to anyone along the way. Do not utter a word until you have brought the boy back to life."

Gaichazi rushed to do his master's bidding, but he was not a worthy disciple. He did not take Elisha's warning seriously. He spoke to people he met on the way and told them where he was going, asking them, "Do you believe that this stick has the power to revive the dead?"

When he arrived at her house, he did exactly what Elisha had told him, but the lad would not budge. When Gaichazi returned to Elisha and told him of his failure, the prophet hurried there himself, climbed up to the attic, shut the door and began praying. "Master of the universe!" he said, "just as

You gave Eliyahu the power to revive the dead, I ask You to grant me that power so that I can revive the lad lying here before me." Elisha then bent over the boy, put his mouth to the lad's mouth, his eyes upon the boy's eyes, his hands upon the small hands. Hashem heard his prayer and restored life to the form on the bed. Suddenly he awoke. Elisha carried him down to his surprised mother who rejoiced upon seeing her son alive.

18

ELISHA SAVES THE JEWISH PEOPLE

Elisha led his people for many years, guiding the G-d-fearing Jews of Israel. He prophesied for them and saved many people in need. One time, as he was walking through a field, he met a group of student prophets and joined them for a brief rest. Because there was a famine in Shomron at this time, people used to scavenge in fields and forests for something to eat. Elisha asked his attendant to cook up a soup for all of them. He took a large pot, filled it with water and put some edible greens into it. Among these greens was one poisonous weed, although the group was not aware of this. When they tasted the soup, however, it was terribly bitter. They spat it out, shouting, "There is death in that pot!" Elisha asked for some flour, put it into the pot of poisoned soup, and suddenly it was no longer bitter or poisonous! Everyone ate their fill and remained unharmed.

Elisha was still sitting in the company of these student prophets when along came a man bringing them twenty loaves of bread. "Divide these up among all the men," Elisha told Gaichazi.

"How can I divide twenty loaves among one hundred men? No one will be satisfied!" he replied.

"Do what you are told! Give out the bread, and let them eat. Thus says Hashem, 'Eat and leave over!'" And that is exactly what happened! Everyone ate his fill from those loaves and even left some over, as Hashem had told Elisha.

Another time, Elisha rescued the student prophets when he went to the forest with them to chop wood. One of their axes fell into the river there, prompting the person who had been wielding it to approach Elisha in distress. "That ax was not even mine," he said. "I borrowed it from a neighbor, but I have no money to buy him another one to replace it! What shall I do?" Elisha broke off a branch, threw it into the water where the ax had gone under, and suddenly the ax floated to the surface. The man hurried to retrieve it.

Sometimes Elisha, even helped out sinners, not because they deserved it, but to demonstrate the greatness of the Creator and show how He guided and loved His people. The king of Aram, who had his eyes on Eretz Yisrael and always sought to seize parts of it, used to send troops to try to capture King Yehoram. But they never succeeded because Elisha always learned, through his divine intuition, where the soldiers were hiding. He was thus able to warn the king in advance. Indeed, his forecasts were so accurate that even the Aramean soldiers recognized his extraordinary power and reported to their king that they would never succeed in capturing King Yehoram as long as Elisha was alive. This angered the king further. Who was this man, who made him a laughingstock? The proud king of Aram sent his best soldiers to catch the Jewish prophet.

The troops searched the country thoroughly until they finally learned that Elisha was hiding out in Dosan. They surrounded the city from all sides. Elisha's aide saw all the soldiers and knowing whom they were seeking, began shouting in panic. But because Elisha did not want the boy's cries to reveal their location, he prayed to Hashem to calm him. Suddenly the youth looked up and saw the mountain beyond the city full of fiery horses and chariots. "All these have come to save us," Elisha reassured him. By this time the troops had discovered where Elisha was and began forming a tight cordon around him. Elisha again prayed to Hashem, begging to be made unrecognizable. The foreign soldiers approached Elisha but did not know who he was. Elisha further fooled them by saying,"The man you are seeking is not here. If you wish, I can lead you to his hiding place." The soldiers thanked him and followed behind. Actually, Elisha had not lied because when he had spoken, he was already outside the city limits and was technically not in Dosan.

Elisha led the soldiers to Shomron. There, in range of the Jewish troops, the Arameans suddenly realized that they had been duped by none other than Elisha himself, but it was too late to escape. King Yehoram asked the prophet if he should kill all the soldiers, but Hashem said to leave them unharmed "These troops did not fall into the hands of the Jewish soldier: through your doing, and you did not take them prisoner Therefore you must not harm them. Just give them som bread and water. Let them eat and drink and return peacefull to their land." The king did as Hashem commanded. Tl soldiers returned to Aram and told their king of all the adventures. This time he finally realized that he would nev succeed in kidnapping King Yehoram or harming the proph of Hashem, and so he left the Jews in peace.

19

NAAMAN'S AFFLICTION

The Aramean army was commanded by Naaman. It was Naaman's arrow that had killed Achav, even though he had not aimed at the king in particular. He was rewarded for this feat by being promoted from simple infantryman to commander. Naaman was wealthy and respected; he had a large household with many servants and maids, one of whom was a Jewish girl captured during a battle.

It happened once that Naaman contracted *tzaraas* (often mistakenly called "leprosy"). His entire body became inflamed with painful sores, but the doctors of Aram were unable to do anything to help him. Seeing her master's terrible suffering, the Jewish maid said to her mistress, "In my country there is a prophet who performs all sorts of wonders. Send your husband to him; he will surely be able to heal him." Naaman and his wife clutched at this hope. After all, neither the doctors nor the gods of his own country had been able to help him.

Naaman went to the king and told him what his Jewish maid had said. "You have my permission to go," the king responded. "I will provide you with a letter of introduction to the king of Israel, asking him to send you to the prophet."

Loaded down with many gifts and the letter of introduction, Naaman went to Yehoram. When the king read the letter, he panicked, "Who am I to guarantee that you can be healed? Am I G-d, Who can heal all? Your king knows well enough that I am helpless as he in this matter. He must be seeking some excuse or provocation to fight; I cannot think of anything else."

News of the ailing commander reached Elisha, who immediately sent a message to the king. "Why did you tear your clothing in panic? Don't you know that Hashem can do anything? Send the man to me, and let me show him and his people that there is, indeed, a prophet in Israel!"

Before Naaman even reached Elisha, the latter sent him a message saying, "Go and bathe in the Jordan River. Immerse yourself seven times, and your *tzoraas* will be healed."

The Aramean commander was furious. "I expected the Jewish prophet to at least come himself to greet me. But what does he do? He sends a message telling me to dip in the Jordan. Am I a fool to believe that this will really heal me? Are the rivers of Aram, Avana and Parpar, not at least as good, if not better? I have bathed in them but have not been healed!" Naaman's men soothed their master and begged him to at least try the holy man's advice. If he had already come this far, why should he not try this? They coaxed and begged him until he finally agreed. Naaman immersed himself seven times in the Jordan and lo! His skin became as smooth as a child's, unblemished and soft. Brimming with joy, the man rushed to Elisha to thank him, exclaiming publicly, "Now I know that there is no god to compare with Hashem, the G-d of Israel!"

20

SIN AND PUNISHMENT

As a sign of his deep appreciation, Naaman came to visit Elisha, heavily leaden with gifts of clothing and silver. But the prophet refused to accept any of these. "The G-d of Israel cured you, not I. I have no right to accept any reward," he said and sent Naaman home. But Gaichazi, Elisha's aide, had seen all the gifts and desired them. As soon as Naaman was gone, he ran after him saying that Elisha had changed his mind and requested two suits and a bar of silver.

Naaman willingly gave these to Gaichazi and continued on his way home. The lad concealed the gifts from his master, but Elisha learned about the deception through his divine intuition. And when Gaichazi returned, he rebuked him angrily, "Sinner! What have you done? Why did you accept the silver and the clothing from Naaman? You know that I did not send you after him. Why did you lie? Since you did so, may you be punished with the very *tzaraas* that afflicted Naaman, to the end of your days!" The words had scarcely left the prophet's mouth when Gaichazi became as white as snow.

Gaichazi deserved such a harsh punishment because he made light of *mitzvos* and did not believe in the resurrection of the dead. On the occasion when Elisha had told him to go and place his staff upon the Shunamite woman's dead son and not to talk to anyone on the way, he had walked along at a leisurely pace, mocking Elisha's instructions to everyone he met. "Do you believe that this stick can revive the dead?" he had said. Not only did Gaichazi sin, but he prevented Elisha's disciples from learning Torah from their master. Whenever they appeared, Gaichazi would station himself outside the door, as if to show that there was no more room inside the *beis midrash*. And so, they would leave disappointed.

After he became leprous, Gaichazi left his master and went to Beis El. There he began worshipping the idols that Yeravam ben Nevat had set up. To draw more people to the idol worship, Gaichazi hung a stone with special magical powers upon the neck of one of the calves. It was able to lift the calf in the air, making people think that the idol had ascended by itself. He also engraved the Ineffable Name of Hashem upon the calf's mouth, enabling it to talk. The calf exclaimed, "I am Hashem your G-d . . . You shall not have any other gods before Me . . ."

From Beis El he went to Damascus. Elisha, who had come seeking Gaichazi to urge him to repent, found him there. Elisha felt himself to blame for the youth's terrible sins, for he had expelled him from his house. But Gaichazi refused to listen to his former master, saying, "Did you not teach me that whoever sins and causes others to sin shall not have a portion in the World to Come? It is too late now, so why should I change my ways?" Heartbroken at the failure of his mission, Elisha returned home while Gaichazi continued to sin. He died without repenting, thereby forfeiting his portion in *Olam Haba*.

Elisha had contact with another Jew who was punished severely for his sin. Once, during a heavy famine, the King of Aram sent his armies to lay siege to the city of Shomron. No one was allowed to enter or leave. The food reserves were soon depleted, and people began to starve. People were so desperate that they stalked the streets looking for anything even barely edible. The king and his commander rode through the streets and saw the people's plight but were powerless to help them. Just then Elisha appeared and exclaimed, "Thus says Hashem: tomorrow at this time you will have so much food that the wheat and barley will be sold for mere pennies."

The commander laughed and said, "I do not believe that. Even if Hashem were to open up the windows of heaven and let food rain down, it would not be enough to satisfy all these hungry people!"

Elisha reacted with anger, "Since you deny Hashem's power and might, you will live to see the prophecy come true, but you will not eat from the plenty!"

The very next day Elisha's prophecy was realized. That night, Hashem confused the Aramean armies and caused them to flee in terror, leaving everything behind. The Jews burst into the abandoned camp and seized all the food that was there. The king's commander stood by the city gates and saw the miracle but was trampled to death when the hungry people stampeded towards the food. Thus was Elisha's word fulfilled to the letter; the doubter saw the vast stores of food but did not get a chance to eat therefrom.

21

RESURRECTION OF THE DEAD

Elisha performed a miracle even in death. There lived a man, Shalum ben Tikva, known for his kindness, charity and hospitality. Each day this man would go to the city gates with a jug full of cool water to give to thirsty travelers. Hashem rewarded this kind man and him and his wife with prophecy.

When Shalum died, he was given a large funeral which the entire city attended. His body was carried aloft on the shoulders of weeping townsmen when suddenly an army came along and frightened the people away. Everyone dispersed, abandoning Shalum's bier on the roadside. The body landed on Elisha's grave and touched the prophet's bones. Suddenly, Shalum came alive. He walked home as if nothing had happened. People could not believe their eyes. They exclaimed, "Hashem has rewarded Shalum measure for measure for his good deeds. Since he revived the poor by feeding them, Hashem has revived him and granted him new life."

But this modest and G-d-fearing man did not think he deserved such a great reward. And the following year, when Hashem blessed him with a son, he called him Chanamel, explaining, "Hashem has given me these extra years for free (*chinam*)." He felt he did not deserve them.

Part Three

Yonah the Prophet

1

HASHEM'S MESSENGER TO NINEVEH

Elisha had many fine disciples, the chief of them being Yonah. Already during his master's lifetime, people sensed that he would one day be a great prophet. It was Yonah whom Elisha sent to anoint Yeihu as king over Israel. Yeihu ben Yehoshafat was the only monarch of the Kingdom of Israel who did not sin and cause others to sin. When Yonah was about to anoint him as king, Elisha first told his disciple, "Thus must you say to the Jewish people: Hashem has sent me to get you to repent. Abandon your gods of wood and stone, and worship Hashem alone! If you do not heed My words, you will suffer bitterly. Jerusalem will be destroyed, and you will be sent into exile." The Jews did take Yonah's threat seriously, and they repented. Seeing their sincerity, Hashem did not punish them.

After a time, the Jews, who were living in peace and harmony upon their land, came to Yonah taunting, "You are a false prophet, for you said that Jerusalem would be destroyed, and we would be exiled. But nothing has happened. We have never lived better. You must have made up those threats by yourself." Yonah was deeply hurt by these words.

Shortly after, Hashem said to Yonah, "Go to Nineveh, the

great city of Ashur, and say thus to its inhabitants: if you do not forsake your evil ways, if you continue to steal and rob, the G-d of Israel shall destroy you."

Upon hearing his assignment from Hashem, Yonah thought, "I know that the people of Nineveh will repent, and then Hashem will have no cause to punish them. Then they, too, will come to me and say that I am a false prophet, a prophet of doom whose predictions never come true. Is it not bad enough that the Jews consider me a false prophet? No!" he decided. "I will not deliver this prophecy to them. I do not want the nations to mock me. I will flee to a foreign country, an impure country where Hashem will not rest His spirit upon me. I will not prophesy against Nineveh."

Without first asking permission from Hashem, Yonah went to the port of Yaffo to find the boat which sailed to distant Tarshish. "The ship left two days ago," he was informed. "It won't be returning for a long time. But while he stood there considering what to do, the ship suddenly appeared on the horizon, heading towards the harbor. Hashem wished to test Yonah to see if he really intended to carry out his plan and had caused high seas to force the sailors back. Yonah boarded the ship at once, thinking that Hashem was not opposed to his traveling to Tarshish. Yonah paid the captain a good deal of money so that the ship would sail immediately.

The next day, when they were out at sea, huge waves started rising up. A storm was raging which nearly capsized the ship. The passengers were puzzled, however, for they could see ships all around them sailing along smoothly as if nothing was happening. Something is strange here, they concluded, and each began praying to his god to save him. The passengers were a varied lot, from different countries, each with his own form of worship. After a brief consultation, they decided, "Let each man pray to his own god. Whichever god answers and saves us all from drowning will become the god of all of us." With both fear and hope, each man took his image and began crying out to his deity. Hours passed, but the waves continued to rage, the storm threatening to kill them all.

Suddenly, the captain remembered that there was another passenger on board. Where was he? He was not among the rest, praying on deck. A thorough search was made until Yonah was discovered in the hold of the ship, fast asleep. He did not know anything about the impending danger. The captain shook him angrily and said, "What's with you, you slumberer! Don't you know that the ship is about to sink and that we are all about to die? Everyone else is on deck, praying desperately, while you sleep peacefully on. Get up and join the rest. Go and pray to your god, perhaps he can save us." When the captain learned that Yonah was a Jew, who worshiped the G-d of the Hebrews, he rejoiced, "I have heard much about your G-d. He is truly mighty and great. Go and pray to Him! Perhaps He will perform miracles for us as He did for your ancestors at the Red Sea."

Yonah understood that he was the cause of the storm. Because he had sought to escape the mission with which Hashem had charged him, he was responsible for the lives of all those aboard ship. Lest innocent people die on account of him, Yonah turned to the captain and said, "I am the cause of your trouble. If you want to save your crew and passengers, you must throw me into the sea. The storm will stop at once."

Everyone who heard this was deeply moved. They were good people and did not wish to harm him. Besides, they did not really believe him.

And so they decided to cast lots. Only when these pointed to Yonah, did they begin to think that he might have spoken the truth. But they still were too kindhearted to consider throwing him into the raging sea. Instead, in order to lighten the ship, they began throwing all of their belongings into the water and tried to row back to shore. Seeing that all their efforts failed, they finally thrust Yonah into the water. As soon as his feet touched the water, the waves quieted down.

They then drew him back into the ship, but the waves reared up higher than before. Once again, they dipped Yonah into the sea, this time up to his navel, and the waves subsided as before. When they pulled him back up on deck, the storm began afresh. The third time, they plunged Yonah into water up to his neck, and all was calm. Now they could not deny that he was the source of all their trouble.

They now held down the prophet and prayed to Hashem, "O G-d of Israel! We do not want to kill this man. We do not know him; we do not know what his sins are or why he has been sentenced to die. He himself tells us to cast him into the water. Since we have no choice, we are doing what he directs." With heavy heart, they finally threw him completely into the water. After he had sunk, the sea became calm and peaceful.

2

YONAH IN THE FISH'S BELLY

During the week of Creation, Hashem made the fish that was to swallow up Yonah. Yonah entered this fish's belly like a man entering a large synagogue. He was able to walk comfortably around inside the fish. A large pearl in the fish's stomach cast light like the sun at noon. The fish's two eyes were like two windows into the sea through which Yonah could look and see what was happening outside. As soon as he was swallowed up, the fish said to Yonah, "You know that the leviathan is the king of fishes. Each day a large fish must go to him to be his meal. Today is my turn. I am going to the leviathan so that he can eat me."

Yonah reassured his fish, "Do not fear. Take me to the leviathan. I will save you from his jaws."

When the fish appeared before the leviathan, Yonah spoke up. "Let me tell you that I entered the sea just to visit you and see where you live." Perplexed, the leviathan asked Yonah why he had done so. Yonah explained, "I wanted to see the great fish which stands in readiness for the feast which Hashem will make for the *tzaddikim* in the latter days. When *Mashiach* comes, I will take a rope and pull you to land where I will slaughter you for that great feast." At these words, the leviathan panicked and fled, sparing the large fish containing Yonah.

When the danger had passed, Yonah said to the fish, "I have saved your life. Now you must repay me. I want you to show me all that exists under the sea, all of the buried treasures hidden in these depths." Willingly, the fish swam about and took Yonah to all parts of the ocean, passing through rivers and seas and showing him the underwater marvels.

Yonah was shown deep pits whose waters the leviathan drank when he was thirsty. When they suddenly felt a warm stream of water shooting past them, the fish explained, "That was caused by the leviathan. His hot breath made the ocean boil." In the depths of the ocean, Yonah was shown Gehinnom and then was taken to the palace of Hashem where he beheld the glory and grandeur of the Creator. Under this majestic palace he saw the foundation stone of the world, the *even hashesiyah*. It was surrounded by people pleading before Hashem. Yonah was puzzled, but the fish explained, "These are the sons of Korach who were swallowed up by the ground. They have been standing here ever since, pleading for mercy for their father."

The great fish led Yonah to the Red Sea and showed him the very spot where the Jews had crossed on dry land upon leaving Egypt. The fish swam about for three days and three nights, showing Yonah all the sights of the seabed. Yonah was so overwhelmed that he forgot where he was and did not even remember to pray to Hashem to remove him from the fish's belly.

Hashem waited for the *tzaddik*'s prayer. When Yonah failed to pray, Hashem became angry at him and said, "I did

Yonah the kindness of providing him with a gigantic fish where he would be comfortable and would not suffer. But he did not pray to me even once. Now I will put him into a smaller fish pregnant with innumerable little fish. He will be so cramped there that he will not forget to pray. He will think of Me and beg to be released."

At once another large fish swam up to the one carrying Yonah and said, "I have been sent directly from Hashem to swallow up Yonah, who is inside you. Spit him out so that I can fulfill my mission. If you refuse, I will swallow both you and the prophet inside you." The fish containing Yonah first demanded proof that Hashem had indeed sent it. "Leviathan, the king of the fish, will testify that I am telling the truth." With these words, both fish swam to the leviathan, who confirmed what the second fish had said. And so the first fish spat Yonah out, and the second fish opened its jaws to swallow him up.

It was indeed cramped inside this pregnant fish. The thousands of fish inside did not let Yonah move around. In his misery, he now cried out to Hashem, begging to be rescued and allowed to reach civilization. "Rescue me from this place," he wept. "Now I know that no one can hide from You; no one can flee from Your decrees. Were I to fly to heaven, there would I find You. Were I to descend to the nethermost depths, there I would find You. Even in the depths of the sea, You can manipulate me as You wish. Save me, Hashem, and return me to a community of human beings." Hashem heard Yonah's prayer but did not answer it before hearing the prophet's promise that he would fulfill Hashem's command. Only then, did Hashem order the fish to spit Yonah out.

The huge fish spat Yonah a great distance, from out at sea all the way to the dry land. When they saw Yonah, his former fellow passengers were aghast. His clothing and hair were burnt from the great heat he had been exposed to inside the fishes. When they heard him relate his marvelous adventures, they were even more impressed. They immediately cast their idols into the sea, saying, "We have no need for these any more now that we have seen who the great G-d is. There is no comparison between His might and the helplessness of our idols." All the people aboard the ship decided to go to Jerusalem where they converted and circumcised themselves.

3
THE PEOPLE OF NINEVEH REPENT

After his rescue from the sea and the two fish, Yonah went directly to Nineveh to prophesy, as Hashem had commanded him. Nineveh was a huge metropolis of half a million inhabitants, all of them valiant. There were twelve enormous markets in the city, each of which held twelve thousand people. Each of its streets had twelve side streets, each of which was made up of twelve courtyards. Each courtyard had twelve houses, each of which housed twelve stalwart men. Each man had twelve sons, valiant like their father.

The prophet Yonah stood in the central square and exclaimed publicly, "In forty days Nineveh will be destroyed unless you repent before Hashem and abandon your evil ways." The prophet's words reached all the corners of the city. When the proclamation reached the ears of Osnapar, King of Ashur, who ruled in Nineveh, he rose from his throne, removed his royal crown, shed his royal raiment and donned sackcloth and ashes. He called to all his countrymen to repent. "Hear ye! Hear ye!" he proclaimed through the city streets. "From this minute on, no one is to eat or drink for three days and three nights until Hashem takes pity on us and repeals the harsh decree."

The people of Nineveh believed Yonah, and wherever the king's decree was publicized, there was general mourning and fasting. People donned sackcloth, put earth upon their heads and prayed to the G-d of Israel. In order to arouse heavenly compassion, they separated cows from their calves and mares from their colts and placed them opposite each other. The neighing and bleating could be heard for miles around. The people of Nineveh prayed, "Look, Hashem, at these unhappy creatures. They are famished; they cry out for their mother's milk. If You show pity on us, we will have pity on them too and will unite each animal with its mother." Then they took their own children, lifted them up high and said, "Look at these children, Hashem. Have they sinned against You? Forgive us for the sake of these innocent children, who have never sinned."

The people of Nineveh went beyond prayer; they also repented in deed. Everyone returned anything he had ever stolen or wrongly taken. Every item of clothing or jewelry which contained anything stolen was taken apart so that mere buttons or beads could be returned to their lawful owners. The king even had his magnificent palace torn down so that he could return the stones and marble that he had seized from his people by force. People who deserved to die for their sins appeared before the courts, begging to be punished. Each person sincerely desired to take the punishment he deserved as long as Hashem would not destroy their city.

A certain man in Nineveh had once bought a plot of land upon which stood some ruins. When he was about to clear the land so that he could build upon it, he discovered a vast treasure buried under the floor of the ruined house. He immediately went to the former owner to hand over the treasure. "All I bought was some land with ruins on it. I did not purchase this treasure."

But the seller said, "I sold you the entire land and all that it contained. The treasure rightfully belongs to you."

Since neither of them wished to benefit from the money, they went to court. The judge told them to put the money aside until they found the rightful owner. The three men made every effort to locate the owner of the treasure and finally succeeded. Residents of Nineveh went to this extent in trying to do what was right. Hashem, Who always waits eagerly for sinners to repent, saw their deeds, heard their prayers and knew that they meant well. He had pity on them and "moved" from His Throne of Justice to His Throne of Mercy, tore up the harsh edit and forgave them.

4

YONAH AND THE KIKAYON

Yonah knew beforehand that Hashem would not destroy the city of Nineveh. When he saw that Hashem had indeed pitied them and accepted their repentance, he fell upon the ground and said, "Master of the universe! I know that I sinned by running away from You. I beg You to forgive me, just as You forgave the people of Nineveh." Hashem heard him and replied, "I have already forgiven you. You really sought to protect My honor. That is why you fled. You did not want people to say that I did not execute My threats, that I put false words into the mouth of My prophet. Therefore I pitied you when you were thrown into the sea and sent the great fish to swallow you. And when you were cramped inside the second fish, I also saved you and brought you back to civilization."

The city of Nineveh was surrounded by a great desert. When the prophet left the city to return home, the sun beat mercilessly down upon his head. Since Yonah was bald and his tattered clothing offered poor protection, he felt faint from the heat. He lay down and fell asleep. But soon, flies, mosquitoes and ants began biting mercilessly. When Hashem beheld his torment, He caused a *kikayon* to spring up at his side. The plentiful leaves of this tree sheltered him from the sun, and the insects all disappeared. When he arose, he rejoiced at the sight of the protective tree by his side.

Hashem now sent a small worm, which gnawed at the tree's roots, causing it to shrivel up suddenly and die. The sun began beating upon him again, and the bothersome insects returned. Yonah was so tormented that he wished he could die. Hashem saw his tears of frustration and asked him why he was weeping. "I am feeling sorry for myself for having lost the protection of the *kikayon* which shriveled up."

Hashem responded, "You are weeping over a tree which you did not plant or nurture, for which you did nothing. It grew all by itself, overnight, and disappeared overnight. Yet you mourn for it. How then shall I not show compassion to the great city of Nineveh and all of its inhabitants? I created them, but you want Me to destroy them just so that you would not appear to be a liar. Should I then have wiped out this city just to protect your honor?"

Seeing things in this light, Yonah felt ashamed and said humbly, "Please, Hashem, G-d of Mercy and Forgiveness, continue to rule the world with mercy."

5

THE END OF THE PEOPLE OF NINEVEH

The people of Nineveh continued along the path of righteousness for another forty years. But then they abandoned Hashem and angered Him exceedingly. They forgot the prophet's warning. Hashem noted their behavior and the city was uprooted and destroyed and all of its inhabitants killed.

מראה מקומות - SOURCES

חלק ז - מלכי יהודה וישראל

א) **התפלגות ממלכת שלמה** - שבת נו, ב; סנהדרין כא, ב. קא-קב; ויק"ר יב,ה; במב"ר יד, ד.

ב) **ירבעם בן נבט מלך ישראל** - סנהדרין קא-קב; זו"ח סוף בראשית, סוף אחרי; שו"ט ה.

ג) **רחבעם בן שלמה** - שבת נו, ב; מלכים א, יב.

ד) **מלכות ירבעם בן נבט** - סנהדרין קא, קב; סע פט"ז; ירושלמי ע"ז פ"א ה"א; ילק"ש קצט, רא; תנחומא תולדות יב, תשא ו; פסדר"כ שקלים פי"ב.

ה) **ירבעם ואיש האלקים** - סנהדרין פט, ב. קב. קד; מלכים א, יג.

ו) **ירבעם ורחבעם** - דברה"י ב, יא-יב. קה"ר ג, יא.

ז) **אביה בן ירבעם** - שכחת לקט משיחו; מגלה עמוקות רנו; מו"ק כח, ב; זו"ח כ,א. נו, א.

ח) **אביה בן רחבעם** - ירושלמי יבמות טז, ה"ו; ב"ר סי"ה כ. עג, ה; סי"ע, פי"ז; מד"יש פי"ח; ויק"ר לג, ה.

ט) **אסא מלך יהודה** - תוספתא סוטה יב, ג; רש"י מלכים א טז, כב; ילק"ש חי"ב עא, קעב; סוטה י, א.

חלק ח - אליהו ואלישע הנביאים

א) **אחאב מלך ישראל** - אי"ר ט; סנהדרין קב. קיג, א; ירושלמי סנהדרין פי"י, ה"ב שו"ט קיז; מד"יש ה; תנחומא מסעי ח; תני"י מסעי ו.

ב) **אליהו ומפתח של גשמים** - סנהדרין קיג, א; ב"ר נ, יא; פסקיר ג, ג; שהש"ר ב, ה; ירושלמי סוכה פג; ילק"ש חי"ב רז, רט.

ג) **אליהו ועובדיהו** - סנהדרין לט, ב; ילק"ש חי"ב, רי; ויק"ר כו, ב.

ד) **אליהו בהר הכרמל** - תנחומא מסעי ח; אי"ר יז; תני"י מסעי ו; במב"ר כג, ט; ילק"ש חי"ב, ריד; ויק"ר לא, ד; שהש"ר ז, ד.

ה) **הר הכרמל** - ב"ר צט, א; מגלה כט א; ילק"ש חי"ב ריד.

ו) **שכר אהבת התורה** - סנהדרין קב, ב; ירושלמי סנהדרין פי"י ה"ב; ויק"ר כו, ח; תנחומא שמות כט; שמו"ר ג,ח; ילק"ש חי"א תרכו; איכ"ר א, מג.

ז) **כרם נבות היזרעלי** - פסקיר כו, ב; ילק"ש חי"ב, רכא; ירושלמי סנהדרין פי"י, ה"ב; פדרייא מג; פסדר"כ, כה; סנהדרין קב, א; מ"כ 31.

ח) **סופו של אחאב** - סנהדרין קב, ב; ילק"ש חי"ב רכב; מגלה ג, א; בי"ק יז, א; מ"כ 31; במב"ר יד, א; תנחומא תשא טו; שהש"ר א, מב.

ט) **אליהו -נביא ה'** - ילק"ש בראשית א, כו; ילק"ר ערך אליהו, מו"ק כו, א; קוה"ר ג; די"א זוטא א; תנחומא פקודי ג; סי"ע פי"ז זו"ח עו; פתיחתא דרו"ר א; ויק"ר לד, ח; אי"ר ה; דבי"י ג, יז.

י) **אליהו מושיע את ישראל** - פדרייא כט, אי"ר ה. גיטין ו, ב; בי"מ נט, ב. פה, ב.

יא) **אליהו בעתיד לבוא** - מנחות מה, א. מו; פסקיר לו, ד; ילק"ש חי"ב תעה, תקצה; סוכה נב, ב.